CHRISTIANITY AND
LIBERALISM

Christianity and Liberalism

BY

J. GRESHAM MACHEN, D.D.

Late Professor of New Testament in Westminster Theological Seminary, Philadelphia

WM. B. EERDMANS PUBLISHING COMPANY

Grand Rapids   Michigan

Reprinted 1996

ISBN 0-8028-1121-3

To

MY MOTHER

PREFACE

On November 3, 1921, the author of the present book delivered before the Ruling Elders' Association of Chester Presbytery an address which was subsequently published in *The Princeton Theological Review*, vol. xx, 1922, pp. 93-117, under the title "Liberalism or Christianity." The interest with which the published address was received has encouraged the author to undertake a more extensive presentation of the same subject. By courtesy of *The Princeton Theological Review*, free use has been made of the address, which may be regarded as the nucleus of the present book. Grateful acknowledgment is also due to the editor of *The Presbyterian* for kind permission to use various brief articles which were published in that journal. The principal divisions of the subject were originally suggested to the author by a conversation which he held in 1921 with the Rev. Paul Martin of Princeton, who has not, however, been consulted as to the method of treatment.

CONTENTS

CHRISTIANITY AND LIBERALISM

CHAPTER I

INTRODUCTION

The purpose of this book is not to decide the religious
issue of the present day, but merely to present the issue as
sharply and clearly as possible, in order that the reader
may be aided in deciding it for himself. Presenting an
issue sharply is indeed by no means a popular business
at the present time; there are many who prefer to fight
their intellectual battles in what Dr. Francis L. Patton
has aptly called a "condition of low visibility." [1] Clear-
cut definition of terms in religious matters, bold facing of
the logical implications of religious views, is by many persons regarded as an impious proceeding. May it not
discourage contribution to mission boards? May it not
hinder the progress of consolidation, and produce a poor
showing in columns of Church statistics? But with such
persons we cannot possibly bring ourselves to agree.
Light may seem at times to be an impertinent intruder,
but it is always beneficial in the end. The type of religion
which rejoices in the pious sound of traditional phrases,
regardless of their meanings, or shrinks from "controversial" matters, will never stand amid the shocks of life.
In the sphere of religion, as in other spheres, the things

---

[1] Francis L. Patton, in the introduction to William Hallock John-
son, *The Christian Faith Under Modern Searchlights*, [1916], p. 7.

about which men are agreed are apt to be the things that are least worth holding; the really important things are the things about which men will fight.

In the sphere of religion, in particular, the present time is a time of conflict; the great redemptive religion which has always been known as Christianity is battling against a totally diverse type of religious belief, which is only the more destructive of the Christian faith because it makes use of traditional Christian terminology. This modern non-redemptive religion is called "modernism" or "liberalism." Both names are unsatisfactory; the latter, in particular, is question-begging. The movement designated as "liberalism" is regarded as "liberal" only by its friends; to its opponents it seems to involve a narrow ignoring of many relevant facts. And indeed the movement is so various in its manifestations that one may almost despair of finding any common name which will apply to all its forms. But manifold as are the forms in which the movement appears, the root of the movement is one; the many varieties of modern liberal religion are rooted in naturalism—that is, in the denial of any entrance of the creative power of God (as distinguished from the ordinary course of nature) in connection with the origin of Christianity. The word "naturalism" is here used in a sense somewhat different from its philosophical meaning. In this non-philosophical sense it describes with fair accuracy the real root of what is called, by what may turn out to be a degradation of an originally noble word, "liberal" religion.

The rise of this modern naturalistic liberalism has not come by chance, but has been occasioned by important changes which have recently taken place in the conditions of life. The past one hundred years have witnessed the beginning of a new era in human history, which may conceivably be regretted, but certainly cannot be ignored, by the most obstinate conservatism. The change is not something that lies beneath the surface and might be visible only to the discerning eye; on the contrary it forces itself upon the attention of the plain man at a hundred points. Modern inventions and the industrialism that has been built upon them have given us in many respects a new world to live in; we can no more remove ourselves from that world than we can escape from the atmosphere that we breathe.

But such changes in the material conditions of life do not stand alone; they have been produced by mighty changes in the human mind, as in their turn they themselves give rise to further spiritual changes. The industrial world of to-day has been produced not by blind forces of nature but by the conscious activity of the human spirit; it has been produced by the achievements of science. The outstanding feature of recent history is an enormous widening of human knowledge, which has gone hand in hand with such perfecting of the instrument of investigation that scarcely any limits can be assigned to future progress in the material realm.

The application of modern scientific methods is almost as broad as the universe in which we live. Though the most palpable achievements are in the sphere of physics and chemistry, the sphere of human life cannot be isolated from the rest, and with the other sciences there has appeared, for example, a modern science of history, which, with psychology and sociology and the like, claims, even if it does not deserve, full equality with its sister sciences. No department of knowledge can maintain its isolation from the modern lust of scientific conquest; treaties of inviolability, though hallowed by all the sanctions of age-long tradition, are being flung ruthlessly to the winds.

In such an age, it is obvious that every inheritance
from the past must be subject to searching criticism; and
as a matter of fact some convictions of the human race
have crumbled to pieces in the test. Indeed, dependence
of any institution upon the past is now sometimes even
regarded as furnishing a presumption, not in favor of it,
but against it. So many convictions have had to be abandoned that men have sometimes come to believe that all
convictions must go.

If such an attitude be justifiable, then no institution is
faced by a stronger hostile presumption than the institution of the Christian religion, for no institution has based
itself more squarely upon the authority of a by-gone age.
We are not now inquiring whether such policy is wise or
historically justifiable; in any case the fact itself is plain,
that Christianity during many centuries has consistently
appealed for the truth of its claims, not merely and not
even primarily to current experience, but to certain ancient books the most recent of which was written some
nineteen hundred years ago. It is no wonder that that
appeal is being criticized to-day; for the writers of the
books in question were no doubt men of their own age,
whose outlook upon the material world, judged by modern standards, must have been of the crudest and most
elementary kind. Inevitably the question arises whether
the opinions of such men can ever be normative for men
of the present day; in other words, whether first-century
religion can ever stand in company with twentieth-century
science.

However the question may be answered, it presents a
serious problem to the modern Church. Attempts are
indeed sometimes made to make the answer easier than at
first sight it appears to be. Religion, it is said, is so
entirely separate from science, that the two, rightly de-

fined, cannot possibly come into conflict. This attempt at separation, as it is hoped the following pages may show, is open to objections of the most serious kind. But what must now be observed is that even if the separation is justifiable it cannot be effected without effort; the removal of the problem of religion and science itself constitutes a problem. For, rightly or wrongly, religion during the centuries has as a matter of fact connected itself with a host of convictions, especially in the sphere of history, which may form the subject of scientific investigation; just as scientific investigators, on the other hand, have sometimes attached themselves, again rightly or wrongly, to conclusions which impinge upon the innermost domain of philosophy and of religion. For example, if any simple Christian of one hundred years ago, or even of to-day, were asked what would become of his religion if history should prove indubitably that no man called Jesus ever lived and died in the first century of our era, he would undoubtedly answer that his religion would fall away. Yet the investigation of events in the first century in Judæa, just as much as in Italy or in Greece, belongs to the sphere of scientific history. In other words, our simple Christian, whether rightly or wrongly, whether wisely or unwisely, has as a matter of fact connected his religion, in a way that to him seems indissoluble, with convictions about which science also has a right to speak. If, then, those convictions, ostensibly religious, which belong to the sphere of science, are not really religious at all, the demonstration of that fact is itself no trifling task. Even if the problem of science and religion reduces itself to the problem of disentangling religion from pseudo-scientific accretions, the seriousness of the problem is not thereby diminished. From every point of view, therefore, the problem in question is the most serious concern of the Church. What is the relation between Christianity and modern culture; may Christianity be maintained in a scientific age?

It is this problem which modern liberalism attempts to solve. Admitting that scientific objections may arise against the particularities of the Christian religion—against the Christian doctrines of the person of Christ, and of redemption through His death and resurrection —the liberal theologian seeks to rescue certain of the general principles of religion, of which these particularities are thought to be mere temporary symbols, and these general principles he regards as constituting "the essence of Christianity."

It may well be questioned, however, whether this method of defence will really prove to be efficacious; for after the apologist has abandoned his outer defences to the enemy and withdrawn into some inner citadel, he will probably discover that the enemy pursues him even there. Modern materialism, especially in the realm of psychology, is not content with occupying the lower quarters of the Christian city, but pushes its way into all the higher reaches of life; it is just as much opposed to the philosophical idealism of the liberal preacher as to the Biblical doctrines that the liberal preacher has abandoned in the interests of peace. Mere concessiveness, therefore, will never succeed in avoiding the intellectual conflict. In the intellectual battle of the present day there can be no "peace without victory"; one side or the other must win.

As a matter of fact, however, it may appear that the figure which has just been used is altogether misleading; it may appear that what the liberal theologian has retained after abandoning to the enemy one Christian doctrine after another is not Christianity at all, but a religion which is so entirely different from Christianity as to be-

long in a distinct category. It may appear further that
the fears of the modern man as to Christianity were
entirely ungrounded, and that in abandoning the embat-
tled walls of the city of God he has fled in needless panic
into the open plains of a vague natural religion only to
fall an easy victim to the enemy who ever lies in ambush
there.

Two lines of criticism, then, are possible with respect
to the liberal attempt at reconciling science and Christianity. Modern liberalism may be criticized (1) on the
ground that it is un-Christian and (2) on the ground that
it is unscientific. We shall concern ourselves here chiefly
with the former line of criticism; we shall be interested in
showing that despite the liberal use of traditional phraseology modern liberalism not only is a different religion
from Christianity but belongs in a totally different class
of religions. But in showing that the liberal attempt at
rescuing Christianity is false we are not showing that
there is no way of rescuing Christianity at all; on the
contrary, it may appear incidentally, even in the present
little book, that it is not the Christianity of the New
Testament which is in conflict with science, but the supposed Christianity of the modern liberal Church, and
that the real city of God, and that city alone, has defences which are capable of warding off the assaults of
modern unbelief. However, our immediate concern is with
the other side of the problem; our principal concern just
now is to show that the liberal attempt at reconciling
Christianity with modern science has really relinquished
everything distinctive of Christianity, so that what remains is in essentials only that same indefinite type of
religious aspiration which was in the world before Christianity came upon the scene. In trying to remove from
Christianity everything that could possibly be objected to

in the name of science, in trying to bribe off the enemy by those concessions which the enemy most desires, the apologist has really abandoned what he started out to defend. Here as in many other departments of life it appears that the things that are sometimes thought to be hardest to defend are also the things that are most worth defending.

In maintaining that liberalism in the modern Church represents a return to an un-Christian and sub-Christian form of the religious life, we are particularly anxious not to be misunderstood. "Un-Christian" in such a connection is sometimes taken as a term of opprobrium. We do not mean it at all as such. Socrates was not a Christian, neither was Goethe; yet we share to the full the respect with which their names are regarded. They tower immeasurably above the common run of men; if he that is least in the Kingdom of Heaven is greater than they, he is certainly greater not by any inherent superiority, but by virtue of an undeserved privilege which ought to make him humble rather than contemptuous.

Such considerations, however, should not be allowed to obscure the vital importance of the question at issue. If a condition could be conceived in which all the preaching of the Church should be controlled by the liberalism which in many quarters has already become preponderant, then, we believe, Christianity would at last have perished from the earth and the gospel would have sounded forth for the last time. If so, it follows that the inquiry with which we are now concerned is immeasurably the most important of all those with which the Church has to deal. Vastly more important than all questions with regard to methods of preaching is the root question as to what it is that shall be preached.

Many, no doubt, will turn in impatience from the inquiry—all those, namely, who have settled the question in such a way that they cannot even conceive of its being reopened. Such, for example, are the pietists, of whom there are still many. "What," they say, "is the need of argument in defence of the Bible? Is it not the Word of God, and does it not carry with it an immediate certitude of its truth which could only be obscured by defence? If science comes into contradiction with the Bible so much the worse for science!" For these persons we have the highest respect, for we believe that they are right in the main point; they have arrived by a direct and easy road at a conviction which for other men is attained only through intellectual struggle. But we cannot reasonably expect them to be interested in what we have to say.

Another class of uninterested persons is much more numerous. It consists of those who have definitely settled the question in the opposite way. By them this little book, if it ever comes into their hands, will soon be flung aside as only another attempt at defence of a position already hopelessly lost. There are still individuals, they will say, who believe that the earth is flat; there are also individuals who defend the Christianity of the Church, miracles and atonement and all. In either case, it will be said, the phenomenon is interesting as a curious example of arrested development, but it is nothing more.

Such a closing of the question, however, whether it approve itself finally or no, is in its present form based upon a very imperfect view of the situation; it is based upon a grossly exaggerated estimate of the achievements of modern science. Scientific investigation, as has already been observed, has certainly accomplished much; it has in many respects produced a new world. But there is another aspect of the picture which should not be ignored. The modern world represents in some respects an enormous improvement over the world in which our ancestors lived; but in other respects it exhibits a lamentable decline. The improvement appears in the physical conditions of life, but in the spiritual realm there is a corresponding loss. The loss is clearest, perhaps, in the realm of art. Despite the mighty revolution which has been produced in the external conditions of life, no great poet is now living to celebrate the change; humanity has suddenly become dumb. Gone, too, are the great painters and the great musicians and the great sculptors. The art that still subsists is largely imitative, and where it is not imitative it is usually bizarre. Even the appreciation of the glories of the past is gradually being lost, under the influence of a utilitarian education that concerns itself only with the production of physical well-being. The "Outline of History" of Mr. H. G. Wells, with its contemptuous neglect of all the higher ranges of human life, is a thoroughly modern book.

This unprecedented decline in literature and art is only one manifestation of a more far-reaching phenomenon; it is only one instance of that narrowing of the range of personality which has been going on in the modern world. The whole development of modern society has tended mightily toward the limitation of the realm of freedom for the individual man. The tendency is most clearly seen in socialism; a socialistic state would mean the reduction to a minimum of the sphere of individual choice. Labor and recreation, under a socialistic government, would both be prescribed, and individual liberty would be gone. But the same tendency exhibits itself to-day even in those communities where the name of socialism is most abhorred. When once the majority has determined that a certain régime is beneficial, that régime without further hesitation is forced ruthlessly upon the individual man. It never seems to occur to modern legislatures that although "welfare" is good, forced welfare may be bad. In other words, utilitarianism is being carried out to its logical conclusions; in the interests of physical well-being the great principles of liberty are being thrown ruthlessly to the winds.

The result is an unparalleled impoverishment of human life. Personality can only be developed in the realm of individual choice. And that realm, in the modern state, is being slowly but steadily contracted. The tendency is making itself felt especially in the sphere of education. The object of education, it is now assumed, is the production of the greatest happiness for the greatest number. But the greatest happiness for the greatest number, it is assumed further, can be defined only by the will of the majority. Idiosyncrasies in education, therefore, it is said, must be avoided, and the choice of schools must be taken away from the individual parent and placed in the hands of the state. The state then exercises its authority through the instruments that are ready to hand, and at once, therefore, the child is placed under the control of psychological experts, themselves without the slightest acquaintance with the higher realms of human life, who proceed to prevent any such acquaintance being gained by those who come under their care. Such a result is being slightly delayed in America by the remnants of Anglo-Saxon individualism, but the signs of the times are all contrary to the maintenance of this half-way position; liberty is certainly held by but a precarious tenure when once its underlying principles have been lost. For a time it looked as though the utilitarianism which came into vogue in the middle of the nineteenth century would be a purely academic matter, without influence upon daily life. But such appearances have proved to be deceptive. The dominant tendency, even in a country like America, which formerly prided itself on its ·freedom from bureaucratic regulation of the details of life, is toward a drab utilitarianism in which all higher aspirations are to be lost.

Manifestations of such a tendency can easily be seen. In the state of Nebraska, for example, a law is now in force according to which no instruction in any school in the state, public or private, is to be given through the medium of a language other than English, and no language other than English is to be studied even as a language until the child has passed an examination before the county superintendent of education showing that the eighth grade has been passed.[1] In other words, no foreign language, apparently not even Latin or Greek, is to be studied until the child is too old to learn it well. It is in this way that modern collectivism deals with a kind of study which is absolutely essential to all genuine mental advance. The minds of the people of Nebraska, and of any other states where similar laws prevail,[2] are to be kept by the power of the state in a permanent condition of arrested development.

It might seem as though with such laws obscurantism had reached its lowest possible depths. But there are depths lower still. In the state of Oregon, on Election Day, 1922, a law was passed by a referendum vote in accordance with which all children in the state are required to attend the public schools. Christian schools and private schools, at least in the all-important lower grades, are thus wiped out of existence. Such laws, which if the present temper of the people prevails will probably

[1] See *Laws, Resolutions* and *Memorials* passed by the Legislature of the State of Nebraska at the Thirty-Seventh Session, 1919, Chapter 249, p. 1019.

[2] Compare, for example, *Legislative Acts* of the General Assembly of Ohio, Vol. cviii, 1919, pp. 614f.; and *Acts and Joint Resolutions* of the General Assembly of Iowa, 1919, Chapter 198, p. 219.

soon be extended far beyond the bounds of one state,[1] mean of course the ultimate destruction of all real education. When one considers what the public schools of America in many places already are—their materialism, their discouragement of any sustained intellectual effort, their encouragement of the dangerous pseudo-scientific fads of experimental psychology—one can only be appalled by the thought of a commonwealth in which there is no escape from such a soul-killing system. But the principle of such laws and their ultimate tendency are far worse than the immediate results.[2] A public-

[1] In Michigan, a bill similar to the one now passed in Oregon recently received an enormous vote at a referendum, and an agitation looking at least in the same general direction is said to be continuing.

[2] The evil principle is seen with special clearness in the so-called "Lusk Laws" in the state of New York. One of these refers to teachers in the public schools. The other provides that "No person, firm, corporation or society shall conduct, maintain or operate any school, institute, class or course of instruction in any subjects whatever without making application for and being granted a license from the university of the state of New York to so conduct, maintain or operate such institute, school, class or course." It is further provided that "A school, institute, class or course licensed as provided in this section shall be subject to visitation by officers and employees of the university of the state of New York." See *Laws of the State of New York*, 1921, Vol. III, Chapter 667, pp. 2049-2051. This law is so broadly worded that it could not possibly be enforced, even by the whole German army in its pre-war efficiency or by all the espionage system of the Czar. The exact measure of enforcement is left to the discretion of officials, and the citizens are placed in constant danger of that intolerable interference with private life which a real enforcement of the provision about "courses of instruction in any subjects whatever" would mean. One of the exemptions is in principle particularly bad. "Nor shall such license be required," the law provides, "by schools now or hereafter established and maintained by a religious denomination or sect well recognized as such at the time this section takes effect." One can certainly rejoice that the existing churches are freed, for the time being, from the menace involved in the law. But in principle the limitation of the exemption to the existing churches really runs counter to the fundamental idea of religious liberty; for it sets up a distinction between established religions and those that are not established. There was always tolerance for established religious bodies, even in the Roman Empire;

school system, in itself, is indeed of enormous benefit to the race. But it is of benefit only if it is kept healthy at every moment by the absolutely free possibility of the competition of private schools. A public-school system, if it means the providing of free education for those who desire it, is a noteworthy and beneficent achievement of modern times; but when once it becomes monopolistic it is the most perfect instrument of tyranny which has yet been devised. Freedom of thought in the middle ages was combated by the Inquisition, but the modern method is far more effective. Place the lives of children in their formative years, despite the convictions of their parents, under the intimate control of experts appointed by the state, force them then to attend schools where the higher aspirations of humanity are crushed out, and where the mind is filled with the materialism of the day, and it is difficult to see how even the remnants of liberty can subsist. Such a tyranny, supported as it is by a perverse technique used as the instrument in destroying human souls, is certainly far more dangerous than the crude tyrannies of the past, which despite their weapons of fire and sword permitted thought at least to be free.

The truth is that the materialistic paternalism of the present day, if allowed to go on unchecked, will rapidly

but religious liberty consists in equal rights for religious bodies that are new. The other exemptions do not remove in the slightest the oppressive character of the law. Bad as the law must be in its immediate effects, it is far more alarming in what it reveals about the temper of the people. A people which tolerates such preposterous legislation upon the statute books is a people that has wandered far away from the principles of American liberty. True patriotism will not conceal the menace, but will rather seek to recall the citizens to those great principles for which our fathers, in America and in England, were willing to bleed and die. There are some encouraging indications that the Lusk Laws may soon be repealed. If they are repealed, they will still serve as a warning that only by constant watchfulness can liberty be preserved.

make of America one huge "Main Street," where spiritual adventure will be discouraged and democracy will be regarded as consisting in the reduction of all mankind to the proportions of the narrowest and least gifted of the citizens. God grant that there may come a reaction, and that the great principles of Anglo-Saxon liberty may be rediscovered before it is too late! But whatever solution be found for the educational and social problems of our own country, a lamentable condition must be detected in the world at large. It cannot be denied that great men are few or non-existent, and that there has been a general contracting of the area of personal life. Material betterment has gone hand in hand with spiritual decline.

Such a condition of the world ought to cause the choice between modernism and traditionalism, liberalism and conservatism, to be approached without any of the prejudice which is too often displayed. In view of the lamentable defects of modern life, a type of religion certainly should not be commended simply because it is modern or condemned simply because it is old. On the contrary, the condition of mankind is such that one may well ask what it is that made the men of past generations so great and the men of the present generation so small. In the midst of all the material achievements of modern life, one may well ask the question whether in gaining the whole world we have not lost our own soul. Are we forever condemned to live the sordid life of utilitarianism? Or is there some lost secret which if rediscovered will restore to mankind something of the glories of the past?

Such a secret the writer of this little book would discover in the Christian religion. But the Christian religion which is meant is certainly not the religion of the modern liberal Church, but a message of divine grace, almost forgotten now, as it was in the middle ages, but destined to burst forth once more in God's good time, in a new Reformation, and bring light and freedom to mankind. What that message is can be made clear, as is the case with all definition, only by way of exclusion, by way of contrast.   In setting forth the current liberalism, now almost dominant in the Church, over against Christianity, we are animated, therefore, by no merely negative or polemic purpose; on the contrary, by showing what Christianity is not we hope to be able to show what Christianity is, in order that men may be led to turn from the weak and beggarly elements and have recourse again to the grace of God.

CHAPTER II

Modern liberalism in the Church, whatever judgment may be passed upon it, is at any rate no longer merely an academic matter. It is no longer a matter merely of theological seminaries or universities. On the contrary its attack upon the fundamentals of the Christian faith is being carried on vigorously by Sunday-School "lesson-helps," by the pulpit, and by the religious press. If such an attack be unjustified, the remedy is not to be found, as some devout persons have suggested, in the abolition of theological seminaries, or the abandonment of scientific theology, but rather in a more earnest search after truth and a more loyal devotion to it when once it is found.

At the theological seminaries and universities, however, the roots of the great issue are more clearly seen than in the world at large; among students the reassuring employment of traditional phrases is often abandoned, and the advocates of a new religion are not at pains, as they are in the Church at large, to maintain an appearance of conformity with the past. But such frankness, we are convinced, ought to be extended to the people as a whole. Few desires on the part of religious teachers have been more harmfully exaggerated than the desire to "avoid giving offence." Only too often that desire has come perilously near dishonesty; the religious teacher, in his heart of hearts, is well aware of the radicalism of his

17

views, but is unwilling to relinquish his place in the hallowed atmosphere of the Church by speaking his whole mind. Against all such policy of concealment or palliation, our sympathies are altogether with those men, whether radicals or conservatives, who have a passion for light.

What then, at bottom, when the traditional phrases have all been stripped away, is the real meaning of the present revolt against the fundamentals of the Christian faith? What, in brief, are the teachings of modern liberalism as over against the teachings of Christianity?

At the outset, we are met with an objection. "Teachings," it is said, "are unimportant; the exposition of the teachings of liberalism and the teachings of Christianity, therefore, can arouse no interest at the present day; creeds are merely the changing expression of a unitary Christian experience, and provided only they express that experience they are all equally good. The teachings of liberalism, therefore, might be as far removed as possible from the teachings of historic Christianity, and yet the two might be at bottom the same."

Such is the way in which expression is often given to the modern hostility to "doctrine." But is it really doctrine as such that is objected to, and not rather one particular doctrine in the interests of another? Undoubtedly, in many forms of liberalism it is the latter alternative which fits the case. There are doctrines of modern liberalism, just as tenaciously and intolerantly upheld as any doctrines that find a place in the historic creeds. Such for example are the liberal doctrines of the universal fatherhood of God and the universal brotherhood of man. These doctrines are, as we shall see, contrary to the doctrines of the Christian religion. But doctrines they are all the same, and as such they require intellectual defence. In seeming to object to all theology, the liberal preacher is often merely objecting to one system of theology in the interests of another. And the desired immunity from theological controversy has not yet been attained. Sometimes, however, the modern objection to doctrine is more seriously meant. And whether the objection be well-founded or not, the real meaning of it should at least be faced. That meaning is perfectly plain. The objection involves an out-and-out skepticism. If all creeds are equally true, then since they are contradictory to one another, they are all equally false, or at least equally uncertain. We are indulging, therefore, in a mere juggling with words. To say that all creeds are equally true, and that they are based upon experience, is merely to fall back upon that agnosticism which fifty years ago was regarded as the deadliest enemy of the Church. The enemy has not really been changed into a friend merely because he has been received within the camp. Very different is the Christian conception of a creed. According to the Christian conception, a creed is not a mere expression of Christian experience, but on the contrary it is a setting forth of those facts upon which experience is based.

But, it will be said, Christianity is a life, not a doctrine. The assertion is often made, and it has an appearance of godliness. But it is radically false, and to detect its falsity one does not even need to be a Christian. For to say that "Christianity is a life" is to make an assertion in the sphere of history. The assertion does not lie in the sphere of ideals ; it is far different from saying that Christianity ought to be a life, or that the ideal religion is a life. The assertion that Christianity is a life is subject to historical investigation exactly as is the assertion that

the Roman Empire under Nero was a free democracy.
Possibly the Roman Empire under Nero would have been
better if it had been a free democracy, but the historical
question is simply whether as a matter of fact it was a
free democracy or no. Christianity is an historical phenomenon, like the Roman Empire, or the Kingdom of
Prussia, or the United States of America. And as an
historical phenomenon it must be investigated on the basis
of historical evidence.

Is it true, then, that Christianity is not a doctrine but
a life? The question can be settled only by an examination of the beginnings of Christianity. Recognition of
that fact does not involve any acceptance of Christian
belief; it is merely a matter of common sense and common
honesty. At the foundation of the life of every corporation is the incorporation paper, in which the objects of
the corporation are set forth. Other objects may be
vastly more desirable than those objects, but if the direc-
tors use the name and the resources of the corporation to
pursue the other objects they are acting *ultra vires* of the
corporation. So it is with Christianity. It is perfectly
conceivable that the originators of the Christian movement had no right to legislate for subsequent generations;
but at any rate they did have an inalienable right to
legislate for all generations that should choose to bear
the name of "Christian." It is conceivable that Christianity may now have to be abandoned, and another religion substituted for it; but at any rate the question
what Christianity is can be determined only by an examination of the beginnings of Christianity.

The beginnings of Christianity constitute a fairly definite historical phenomenon. The Christian movement
originated a few days after the death of Jesus of Nazareth. It is doubtful whether anything that preceded the

death of Jesus can be called Christianity. At any rate, if Christianity existed before that event, it was Christianity only in a preliminary stage. The name originated after the death of Jesus, and the thing itself was also something new. Evidently there was an important new beginning among the disciples of Jesus in Jerusalem after the crucifixion. At that time is to be placed the beginning of the remarkable movement which spread out from Jerusalem into the Gentile world—the movement which is called Christianity.

About the early stages of this movement definite historical information has been preserved in the Epistles of Paul, which are regarded by all serious historians as genuine products of the first Christian generation. The writer of the Epistles had been in direct communication with those intimate friends of Jesus who had begun the Christian movement in Jerusalem, and in the Epistles he makes it abundantly plain what the fundamental character of the movement was.

But if any one fact is clear, on the basis of this evidence, it is that the Christian movement at its inception was not just a way of life in the modern sense, but a way of life founded upon a message. It was based, not upon mere feeling, not upon a mere program of work, but upon an account of facts. In other words it was based upon doctrine.

Certainly with regard to Paul himself there should be no debate; Paul certainly was not indifferent to doctrine; on the contrary, doctrine was the very basis of his life. His devotion to doctrine did not, it is true, make him incapable of a magnificent tolerance. One notable example of such tolerance is to be found during his imprisonment at Rome, as attested by the Epistle to the Philippians. Apparently certain Christian teachers at

Rome had been jealous of Paul's greatness. As long as he had been at liberty they had been obliged to take a secondary place; but now that he was in prison, they seized the supremacy. They sought to raise up affliction for Paul in his bonds; they preached Christ even of envy and strife. In short, the rival preachers made of the preaching of the gospel a means to the gratification of low personal ambition; it seems to have been about as mean a piece of business as could well be conceived. But Paul was not disturbed. "Whether in pretence, or in truth," he said, "Christ is preached; and I therein do rejoice, yea, and will rejoice" (Phil. i. 18). The way in which the preaching was being carried on was wrong, but the message itself was true; and Paul was far more interested in the content of the message than in the manner of its presentation. It is impossible to conceive a finer piece of broad-minded tolerance.

But the tolerance of Paul was not indiscriminate. He displayed no tolerance, for example, in Galatia. There, too, there were rival preachers. But Paul had no tolerance for them. "But though we," he said, "or an angel from heaven, preach any other gospel unto you than that which we have preached unto you, let him be accursed" (Gal. i. 8). What is the reason for the difference in the apostle's attitude in the two cases? What is the reason for the broad tolerance in Rome, and the fierce anathemas in Galatia? The answer is perfectly plain. In Rome, Paul was tolerant, because there the content of the message that was being proclaimed by the rival teachers was true; in Galatia he was intolerant, because there the content of the rival message was false. In neither case did personalities have anything to do with Paul's attitude. No doubt the motives of the Judaizers in Galatia were far from pure. and in an incidental way Paul does point out their impurity. But that was not the ground of his opposition. The Judaizers no doubt were morally far from perfect, but Paul's opposition to them would have been exactly the same if they had all been angels from heaven. His opposition was based altogether upon the falsity of their teaching; they were substituting for the one true gospel a false gospel which was no gospel at all. It never occurred to Paul that a gospel might be true for one man and not for another; the blight of pragmatism had never fallen upon his soul. Paul was convinced of the objective truth of the gospel message, and devotion to that truth was the great passion of his life. Christianity for Paul was not only a life, but also a doctrine, and logically the doctrine came first.[1]

But what was the difference between the teaching of Paul and the teaching of the Judaizers? What was it that gave rise to the stupendous polemic of the Epistle to the Galatians? To the modern Church the difference would have seemed to be a mere theological subtlety. About many things the Judaizers were in perfect agreement with Paul. The Judaizers believed that Jesus was the Messiah; there is not a shadow of evidence that they objected to Paul's lofty view of the person of Christ. Without the slightest doubt, they believed that Jesus had really risen from the dead. They believed, moreover, that faith in Christ was necessary to salvation. But the trouble was, they believed that something else was also necessary; they believed that what Christ had done needed to be pieced out by the believer's own effort to keep the Law. From the

---

[1] See *The Origin of Paul's Religion,* 1921, p. 168. It is not maintained that doctrine for Paul comes *temporally* before life, but only that it comes *logically* first. Here is to be found the answer to the objection which Dr. Lyman Abbott raised against the assertion in *The Origin of Paul's Religion.* See *The Outlook,* vol. 132, 1922, pp. 104f.

modern point of view the difference would have seemed to
be very slight.   Paul as well as the Judaizers believed that
the keeping of the law of God, in its deepest import, is
inseparably connected with faith.   The difference concerned only the logical—not even, perhaps, the temporal
—order of three steps.   Paul said that a man (1) first
believes on Christ, (2) then is justified before God, (3)
then immediately proceeds to keep God's law.   The Judaizers said that a man (1) believes on Christ and (2) keeps
the law of God the best he can, and then (3) is justified.
The difference would seem to modern "practical" Christians to be a highly subtle and intangible matter, hardly
worthy of consideration at all in view of the large measure
of agreement in the practical realm.   What a splendid
cleaning up of the Gentile cities it would have been if the
Judaizers had succeeded in extending to those cities the
observance of the Mosaic law, even including the unfortunate ceremonial observances!   Surely Paul ought to
have made common cause with teachers who were so nearly
in agreement with him; surely he ought to have applied
to them the great principle of Christian unity.

As a matter of fact, however, Paul did nothing of the
kind; and only because he (and others) did nothing of
the kind does the Christian Church exist to-day.   Paul
saw very clearly that the difference between the Judaizers
and himself was the difference between two entirely distinct types of religion; it was the difference between a
religion of merit and a religion of grace.   If Christ provides only a part of our salvation, leaving us to provide
the rest, then we are still hopeless under the load of sin.
For no matter how small the gap which must be bridged
before salvation can be attained, the awakened conscience
sees clearly that our wretched attempt at goodness is
insufficient even to bridge that gap.   The guilty soul

enters again into the hopeless reckoning with God, to determine whether we have really done our part. And thus we groan again under the old bondage of the law. Such an attempt to piece out the work of Christ by our own merit, Paul saw clearly, is the very essence of unbelief; Christ will do everything or nothing, and the only hope is to throw ourselves unreservedly on His mercy and trust Him for all.

Paul certainly was right. The difference which divided him from the Judaizers was no mere theological subtlety, but concerned the very heart and core of the religion of Christ. "Just as I am without one plea, But that Thy blood was shed for me"—that was what Paul was contending for in Galatia; that hymn would never have been written if the Judaizers had won. And without the thing which that hymn expresses there is no Christianity at all.

Certainly, then, Paul was no advocate of an undogmatic religion; he was interested above everything else in the objective and universal truth of his message. So much will probably be admitted by serious historians, no matter what their own personal attitude toward the religion of Paul may be. Sometimes, indeed, the modern liberal preacher seeks to produce an opposite impression by quoting out of their context words of Paul which he interprets in a way as far removed as possible from the original sense. The truth is, it is hard to give Paul up. The modern liberal desires to produce upon the minds of simple Christians (and upon his own mind) the impression of some sort of continuity between modern liberalism and the thought and life of the great Apostle. But such an impression is altogether misleading. Paul was not interested merely in the ethical principles of Jesus; he was not interested merely in general principles of religion or of ethics. On the contrary, he was interested in the redeem-

ing work of Christ and its effect upon us.　His pr
interest was in Christian doctrine, and Christian do
not merely in its presuppositions but at its centre
Christianity is to be made independent of doctrine, then
Paulinism must be removed from Christianity root and
branch.

But what of that?　Some men are not afraid of the conclusion.　If Paulinism must be removed, they say, we can
get along without it.　May it not turn out that in introducing a doctrinal element into the life of the Church Paul
was only perverting a primitive Christianity which was
as independent of doctrine as even the modern liberal
preacher could desire?

This suggestion is clearly overruled by the historical
evidence.　The problem certainly cannot be solved in so
easy a way.　Many attempts have indeed been made to
separate the religion of Paul sharply from that of the
primitive Jerusalem Church; many attempts have been
made to show that Paul introduced an entirely new principle into the Christian movement or even was the founder
of a new religion.[1]　But all such attempts have resulted
in failure.　The Pauline Epistles themselves attest a
fundamental unity of principle between Paul and the original companions of Jesus, and the whole early history of
the Church becomes unintelligible except on the basis of
such unity.　Certainly with regard to the fundamentally
doctrinal character of Christianity Paul was no inno-
vator.　The fact appears in the whole character of Paul's
relationship to the Jerusalem Church as it is attested by
the Epistles, and it also appears with startling clearness
in the precious passage in I Cor. xv. 3-7, where Paul sum-
marizes the tradition which he had received from the

---

[1] Some account of these attempts has been given by the presen
writer in *The Origin of Paul's Religion*, 1921.

primitive Church. What is it that forms the content of that primitive teaching? Is it a general principle of the fatherliness of God or the brotherliness of man? Is it a vague admiration for the character of Jesus such as that which prevails in the modern Church? Nothing could be further from the fact. "Christ died for our sins," said the primitive disciples, "according to the Scriptures; he was buried; he has been raised on the third day according to the Scriptures." From the beginning, the Christian gospel, as indeed the name "gospel" or "good news" implies, consisted in an account of something that had happened. And from the beginning, the meaning of the happening was set forth; and when the meaning of the happening was set forth then there was Christian doctrine. "Christ died"—that is history; "Christ died for our sins"—that is doctrine. Without these two elements, joined in an absolutely indissoluble union, there is no Christianity.

It is perfectly clear, then, that the first Christian missionaries did not simply come forward with an exhortation; they did not say: "Jesus of Nazareth lived a wonderful life of filial piety, and we call upon you our hearers to yield yourselves, as we have done, to the spell of that life." Certainly that is what modern historians would have expected the first Christian missionaries to say, but it must be recognized that as a matter of fact they said nothing of the kind. Conceivably the first disciples of Jesus, after the catastrophe of His death, might have engaged in quiet meditation upon His teaching. They might have said to themselves that "Our Father which art in heaven" was a good way of addressing God even though the One who had taught them that prayer was dead. They might have clung to the ethical principles of Jesus and cherished the vague hope that the One who

enunciated such principles had some personal existence
beyond the grave. Such reflections might have seemed
very natural to the modern man. But to Peter, James
and John they certainly never occurred. Jesus had raised
in them high hopes; those hopes were destroyed by the
Cross; and reflections on the general principles of religion
and ethics were quite powerless to revive the hopes again.
The disciples of Jesus had evidently been far inferior to
their Master in every possible way; they had not understood His lofty spiritual teaching, but even in the hour of
solemn crisis had quarreled over great places in the approaching Kingdom. What hope was there that such
men could succeed where their Master had failed? Even
when He had been with them, they had been powerless;
and now that He was taken from them, what little power
they may have had was gone.[1]

Yet those same weak, discouraged men, within a few
days after the death of their Master, instituted the most
important spiritual movement that the world has ever
seen. What had produced the astonishing change? What
had transformed the weak and cowardly disciples into the
spiritual conquerors of the world? Evidently it was not
the mere memory of Jesus' life, for that was a source of
sadness rather than of joy. Evidently the disciples of
Jesus, within the few days between the crucifixion and
the beginning of their work in Jerusalem, had received
some new equipment for their task. What that new
equipment was, at least the outstanding and external
element in it (to say nothing of the endowment which
Christian men believe to have been received at Pentecost),
is perfectly plain. The great weapon with which the
disciples of Jesus set out to conquer the world was not

[1] Compare *History and Faith*, 1915 (reprinted from *Princeton
Theological Review* for July, 1915), pp. 10f.

a mere comprehension of eternal principles; it was an historical message, an account of something that had recently happened, it was the message, "He is risen." [1] But the message of the resurrection was not isolated. It was connected with the death of Jesus, seen now to be not a failure but a triumphant act of divine grace; it was connected with the entire appearance of Jesus upon earth. The coming of Jesus was understood now as an act of God by which sinful men were saved. The primitive Church was concerned not merely with what Jesus had said, but also, and primarily, with what Jesus had done. The world was to be redeemed through the proclamation of an event. And with the event went the meaning of the event; and the setting forth of the event with the meaning of the event was doctrine. These two elements are always combined in the Christian message. The narration of the facts is history; the narration of the facts with the meaning of the facts is doctrine. "Suffered under Pontius Pilate, was crucified, dead and buried"—that is history. "He loved me and gave Himself for me"—that is doctrine. Such was the Christianity of the primitive Church.

"But," it may be said, "even if the Christianity of the primitive Church was dependent upon doctrine, we may still emancipate ourselves from such dependence; we may appeal from the primitive Church to Jesus Himself. It has already been admitted that if doctrine is to be abandoned Paul must be abandoned; it may now be admitted that if doctrine is to be abandoned, even the primitive Jerusalem Church, with its message of the resurrection, must be abandoned. But possibly we can still find in Jesus Himself the simple, non-doctrinal religion that we

---

[1] Compare *A Rapid Survey of the Literature and History of New Testament Times*, published by the Presbyterian Board of Publication and Sabbath School Work, Student's Text Book, pp. 42f.

desire." Such is the real meaning of the modern slogan, "Back to Christ."

Must we really take such a step as that? It would certainly be an extraordinary step. A great religion derived its power from the message of the redeeming work of Christ; without that message Jesus and His disciples would soon have been forgotten. The same message, with its implications, has been the very heart and soul of the Christian movement throughout the centuries. Yet we are now asked to believe that the thing that has given Christianity its power all through the centuries was a blunder, that the originators of the movement misunderstood radically the meaning of their Master's life and work, and that it has been left to us moderns to get the first inkling of the initial mistake. Even if this view of the case were correct, and even if Jesus Himself taught a religion like that of modern liberalism, it would still be doubtful whether such a religion could rightly be called Christianity; for the name Christian was first applied only after the supposed decisive change had taken place, and it is very doubtful whether a name which through nineteen centuries has been so firmly attached to one religion ought now suddenly to be applied to another. If the first disciples of Jesus really departed so radically from their Master, then the better terminology would probably lead us to say simply that Jesus was not the founder of Christianity, but of a simple, non-doctrinal religion, long forgotten, but now rediscovered by modern men. Even so, the contrast between liberalism and Christianity would still appear.

But as a matter of fact, such a strange state of affairs does not prevail at all. It is not true that in basing Christianity upon an event the disciples of Jesus were departing from the teaching of their Master. For cer-

tainly Jesus Himself did the same thing. Jesus did not
content Himself with enunciating general principles of
religion and ethics; the picture of Jesus as a sage similar
to Confucius, uttering wise maxims about conduct, may
satisfy Mr. H. G. Wells, as he trips along lightly over the
problems of history, but it disappears so soon as one
engages seriously in historical research. "Repent," said
Jesus, "for the Kingdom of Heaven is at hand." The
gospel which Jesus proclaimed in Galilee consisted in the
proclamation of a coming Kingdom. But clearly Jesus
regarded the coming of the Kingdom as an event, or as a
series of events. No doubt He also regarded the Kingdom
as a present reality in the souls of men; no doubt He
represented the Kingdom in one sense as already present.
We shall not really succeed in getting along without this
aspect of the matter in our interpretation of Jesus' words.
But we shall also not get along without the other aspect,
according to which the coming of the Kingdom depended
upon definite and catastrophic events. But if Jesus regarded the coming of the Kingdom as dependent upon a
definite event, then His teaching was similar at the decisive point to that of the primitive Church; neither He
nor the primitive Church enunciated merely general and
permanent principles of religion; both of them, on the
contrary, made the message depend upon something that
happened. Only, in the teaching of Jesus the happening
was represented as being still in the future, while in
that of the Jerusalem Church the first act of it at least
lay already in the past. Jesus proclaimed the event as
coming; the disciples proclaimed part of it at least as
already past; but the important thing is that both Jesus
and the disciples did proclaim an event. Jesus was certainly not a mere enunciator of permanent truths, like the
modern liberal preacher; on the contrary He was

conscious of standing at the turning-point of the ages, when what had never been was now to come to be.

But Jesus announced not only an event; He announced also the meaning of the event. It is natural, indeed, that the full meaning could be made clear only after the event had taken place. If Jesus really came, then, to announce, and to bring about, an event, the disciples were not departing from His purpose, if they set forth the meaning of the event more fully than it could be set forth during the preliminary period constituted by the earthly ministry of their Master. But Jesus Himself, though by way of prophecy, did set forth the meaning of the great happening that was to be at the basis of the new era.

Certainly He did so, and grandly, if the words attributed to Him in all of the Gospels are really His. But even if the Fourth Gospel be rejected, and even if the most radical criticism be applied to the other three, it will still be impossible to get rid of this element in Jesus' teaching. The significant words attributed to Jesus at the Last Supper with regard to His approaching death, and the utterance of Jesus in Mk. x. 45 ("The Son of Man came not to be ministered unto but to minister, and to give His life a ransom for many"), have indeed been the subject of vigorous debate. It is difficult to accept such words as authentic and yet maintain the modern view of Jesus at all. Yet it is also difficult to get rid of them on any critical theory. What we are now concerned with, however, is something more general than the authenticity even of these precious words. What we are now concerned to observe is that Jesus certainly did not content Himself with the enunciation of permanent moral principles; He certainly did announce an approaching event; and He certainly did not announce the event without giving some account of its meaning. But when He gave an account of the meaning of the event, no matter how brief that account may have been, He was overstepping the line that separates an undogmatic religion, or even a dogmatic religion that teaches only eternal principles, from one that is rooted in the significance of definite historical facts; He was placing a great gulf between Himself and the philosophic modern liberalism which today incorrectly bears His name.

In another way also the teaching of Jesus was rooted in doctrine. It was rooted in doctrine because it depended upon a stupendous presentation of Jesus' own Person. The assertion is often made, indeed, that Jesus kept His own Person out of His gospel, and came forward merely as the supreme prophet of God. That assertion lies at the very root of the modern liberal conception of the life of Christ. But common as it is, it is radically false. And it is interesting to observe how the liberal historians themselves, so soon as they begin to deal seriously with the sources, are obliged to admit that the real Jesus was not all that they could have liked Jesus to be. A Houston Stewart Chamberlain,[1] indeed, can construct a Jesus who was the advocate of a pure, "formless," non-doctrinal religion; but trained historians, despite their own desires, are obliged to admit that there was an element in the real Jesus which refuses to be pressed into any such mould. There is to the liberal historians, as Heitmüller has significantly said, "something almost uncanny" about Jesus.[2]

This "uncanny" element in Jesus is found in His Messianic consciousness. The strange fact is that this pure teacher of righteousness appealed to by modern liberalism, this classical exponent of the non-doctrinal religion

[1] *Mensch und Gott*, 1921. Compare the review in *Princeton Theological Review*, xx, 1922, pp. 327-329.
[2] Heitmüller, *Jesus*, 1913, p. 71. See *The Origin of Paul's Religion*, 1921, p. 157.

which is supposed to underlie all the historical religions as
the irreducible truth remaining after the doctrinal accretions have been removed—the strange fact is that this
supreme revealer of eternal truth supposed that He was
to be the chief actor in a world catastrophe and was to
sit in judgment upon the whole earth. Such is the stupendous form in which Jesus applied to Himself the
category of Messiahship.

It is interesting to observe how modern men have dealt
with the Messianic consciousness of Jesus. Some, like
Mr. H. G. Wells, have practically ignored it. Without
discussing the question whether it be historical or not they
have practically treated it as though it did not exist, and
have not allowed it to disturb them at all in their con-
struction of the sage of Nazareth. The Jesus thus reconstructed may be useful as investing modern programs
with the sanctity of His hallowed name; Mr. Wells may
find it edifying to associate Jesus with Confucius in a
brotherhood of beneficent vagueness. But what ought to
be clearly understood is that such a Jesus has nothing to
do with history. He is a purely imaginary figure, a symbol and not a fact.

Others, more seriously, have recognized the existence
of the problem, but have sought to avoid it by denying
that Jesus ever thought that He was the Messiah, and by
supporting their denial, not by mere assertions, but by
a critical examination of the sources. Such was the
effort, for example, of W. Wrede,[1] and a brilliant effort
it was. But it has resulted in failure. The Messianic
consciousness of Jesus is not merely rooted in the sources
considered as documents, but it lies at the very basis of
the whole edifice of the Church. If, as J. Weiss has
pertinently said, the disciples before the crucifixion had

[1] *Das Messiasgeheimnis in den Evangelien,* 1901.

merely been told that the Kingdom of God was coming, if
Jesus had really kept altogether in the background His
own part in the Kingdom, then why when despair finally
gave place to joy did the disciples not merely say, "Despite Jesus' death, the Kingdom that He foretold will
truly come"? Why did they say rather, "Despite His
death, He is the Messiah"?[1] From no point of view,
then, can the fact be denied that Jesus did claim to be the
Messiah—neither from the point of view of acceptance of
the Gospel witness as a whole, nor from the point of view
of modern naturalism.

And when the Gospel account of Jesus is considered
closely, it is found to involve the Messianic consciousness
throughout. Even those parts of the Gospels which have
been regarded as most purely ethical are found to be based
altogether upon Jesus' lofty claims. The Sermon on the
Mount is a striking example. It is the fashion now to
place the Sermon on the Mount in contrast with the rest
of the New Testament. "We will have nothing to do with
theology," men say in effect, "we will have nothing to do
with miracles, with atonement, or with heaven or with hell.
For us the Golden Rule is a sufficient guide of life; in the
simple principles of the Sermon on the Mount we discover
a solution of all the problems of society." It is indeed
rather strange that men can speak in this way. Certainly
it is rather derogatory to Jesus to assert that never except in one brief part of His recorded words did He say
anything that is worth while. But even in the Sermon on
the Mount there is far more than some men suppose. Men
say that it contains no theology; in reality it contains
theology of the most stupendous kind. In particular, it

[1] J. Weiss, "Das Problem der Entstehung des Christentums," in
Archiv für Religionswissenschaft, xvi. 1913, p. 456. See *The Origin
of Paul's Religion*, 1921, p. 156.

contains the loftiest possible presentation of Jesus' own Person. That presentation appears in the strange note of authority which pervades the whole discourse; it appears in the recurrent words, "But I say unto you." Jesus plainly puts His own words on an equality with what He certainly regarded as the divine words of Scripture; He claimed the right to legislate for the Kingdom of God. Let it not be objected that this note of authority involves merely a prophetic consciousness in Jesus, a mere right to speak in God's name as God's Spirit might lead. For what prophet ever spoke in this way? The prophets said, "Thus saith the Lord," but Jesus said, "I say." We have no mere prophet here, no mere humble exponent of the will of God; but a stupendous Person speaking in a manner which for any other person would be abominable and absurd. The same thing appears in the passage Matt. vii. 21-23: "Not everyone who says to me Lord, Lord, shall enter into the Kingdom of Heaven, but he who does the will of my Father who is in heaven. Many shall say to me in that day: Lord, Lord, have we not prophesied in thy name, and in thy name cast out demons, and in thy name done many mighty works? And then I shall confess to them, 'I never knew you; depart from me, ye that work lawlessness.'" This passage is in some respects a favorite with modern liberal teachers; for it is interpreted—falsely, it is true, yet plausibly—as meaning that all that a man needs to attain standing with God is an approximately right performance of his duties to his fellow-men, and not any assent to a creed or even any direct relation to Jesus. But have those who quote the passage so triumphantly in this way ever stopped to reflect upon the other side of the picture—upon the stupendous fact that in this same passage the eternal destinies of men are made dependent upon the word of Jesus? Jesus here rep-

resents Himself as seated on the judgment-seat of all the
earth, separating whom He will forever from the bliss that
is involved in being present with Him. Could anything be
further removed than such a Jesus from the humble
teacher of righteousness appealed to by modern liberalism? Clearly it is impossible to escape from theology,
even in the chosen precincts of the Sermon on the Mount.
A stupendous theology, with Jesus' own Person at the
centre of it, is the presupposition of the whole teaching.

But may not that theology still be removed? May we
not get rid of the bizarre, theological element which has
intruded itself even into the Sermon on the Mount, and
content ourselves merely with the ethical portion of the
discourse? The question, from the point of view of modern liberalism, is natural. But it must be answered with
an emphatic negative. For the fact is that the ethic of
the discourse, taken by itself, will not work at all. The
Golden Rule furnishes an example. "Do unto others as
you would have others do unto you"—is that rule a rule
of universal application, will it really solve all the problems of society? A little experience shows that such is
not the case. Help a drunkard to get rid of his evil habit,
and you will soon come to distrust the modern interpretation of the Golden Rule. The trouble is that the drunkard's companions apply the rule only too well; they do
unto him exactly what they would have him do unto them
—by buying him a drink. The Golden Rule becomes a
powerful obstacle in the way of moral advance. But the
trouble does not lie in the rule itself; it lies in the modern
interpretation of the rule. The error consists in suppos-
ing that the Golden Rule, with the rest of the Sermon on
the Mount, is addressed to the whole world. As a matter
of fact the whole discourse is expressly addressed to
Jesus' disciples; and from them the great world outside is

distinguished in the plainest possible way. The persons
to whom the Golden Rule is addressed are persons in whom
a great change has been wrought—a change which fits
them for entrance into the Kingdom of God. Such persons will have pure desires; they, and they only, can
safely do unto others as they would have others do unto
them, for the things that they would have others do unto
them are high and pure.

So it is with the whole of the discourse. The new law of
the Sermon on the Mount, in itself, can only produce
despair. Strange indeed is the complacency with which
modern men can say that the Golden Rule and the high
ethical principles of Jesus are all that they need. In
reality, if the requirements for entrance into the Kingdom
of God are what Jesus declares them to be, we are all
undone; we have not even attained to the external righteousness of the scribes and Pharisees, and how shall we
attain to that righteousness of the heart which Jesus
demands? The Sermon on the Mount, rightly interpreted,
then, makes man a seeker after some divine means of salvation by which entrance into the Kingdom can be obtained. Even Moses was too high for us; but before this
higher law cf Jesus who shall stand without being condemned? The Sermon on the Mount, like all the rest of
the New Testament, really leads a man straight to the
foot of the Cross.

Even the disciples, to whom the teaching of Jesus was
first addressed, knew well that they needed more than
guidance in the way that they should go. It is only a
superficial reading of the Gospels that can find in the relation which the disciples sustained to Jesus a mere relation
of pupil to Master. When Jesus said, "Come unto me, all
ye that labour and are heavy laden, and I will give you
rest," he was speaking not as a philosopher calling pupils

to his school; but as One who was in possession of rich stores of divine grace. And this much at least the disciples knew. They knew well in their heart of hearts that they had no right to stand in the Kingdom; they knew that only Jesus could win them entrance there. They did not yet know fully how Jesus could make them children of God; but they did know that He could do it and He alone. And in that trust all the theology of the great Christian creeds was in expectation contained.

At this point, an objection may arise. May we not—the modern liberal will say—may we not now return to that simple trust of the disciples? May we not cease to ask *how* Jesus saves; may we not simply leave the way to Him? What need is there, then, of defining "effectual calling," what need of enumerating "justification, adoption and sanctification and the several benefits which in this life do either accompany or flow from them"? What need even of rehearsing the steps in the saving work of Christ as they were rehearsed by the Jerusalem Church; what need of saying that "Christ died for our sins according to the Scriptures, that he was buried, that he has been raised on the third day according to the Scriptures"? Should not our trust be in a Person rather than in a message; in Jesus, rather than in what Jesus did; in Jesus' character rather than in Jesus' death?

Plausible words these are—plausible, and pitifully vain. Can we really return to Galilee; are we really in the same situation as those who came to Jesus when He was on earth? Can we hear Him say to us, "Thy sins are forgiven thee"? These are serious questions, and they cannot possibly be ignored. The plain fact is that Jesus of Nazareth died these nineteen hundred years ago. It was possible for the men of Galilee in the first century to trust Him; for to them He extended His aid. For them, life's problem was easy. They needed only to push in through the crowd or be lowered through some Capernaum roof, and the long search was over. But we are separated by nineteen centuries from the One who alone could give us aid. How can we bridge the gulf of time that separates us from Jesus?

Some persons would bridge the gulf by the mere use of the historical imagination. "Jesus is not dead," we are told, "but lives on through His recorded words and deeds; we do not need even to believe it all; even a part is sufficient; the wonderful personality of Jesus shines out clear from the Gospel story. Jesus, in other words, may still be known; let us simply—without theology, without controversy, without inquiry about miracles—abandon ourselves to His spell, and He will heal us."

There is a certain plausibility about that. It may readily be admitted that Jesus lives on in the Gospel record. In that narrative we see not merely a lifeless picture, but receive the impression of a living Person. We can still, as we read, share the astonishment of those who listened to the new teaching in the synagogue at Capernaum. We can sympathize with the faith and devotion of the little band of disciples who would not leave Him when others were offended at the hard saying. We feel a sympathetic thrill of joy at the blessed relief which was given to those who were ill in body and in mind. We can appreciate the wonderful love and compassion of Him who was sent to seek and to save that which was lost. A wonderful story it is indeed—not dead, but pulsating with life at every turn.

Certainly the Jesus of the Gospels is a real, a living Person. But that is not the only question. We are going forward far too fast. Jesus lives in the Gospels—so much may freely be admitted—but we of the twentieth century,

how may we come into vital relation to Him? He died
nineteen hundred years ago. The life which He now lives
in the Gospels is simply the old life lived over and over
again. And in that life we have no place; in that life we
are spectators, not actors. The life which Jesus lives in
the Gospels is after all for us but the spurious life of the
stage. We sit silent in the playhouse and watch the
absorbing Gospel drama of forgiveness and healing and
love and courage and high endeavor; in rapt attention
we follow the fortunes of those who came to Jesus laboring
and heavy laden and found rest. For a time our own
troubles are forgotten. But suddenly the curtain falls,
with the closing of the book, and out we go again into the
cold humdrum of our own lives. Gone are the warmth and
gladness of an ideal world, and "in their stead a sense of
real things comes doubly strong." We are no longer living over again the lives of Peter and James and John.
Alas, we are living our own lives once more, with our own
problems and our own misery and our own sin. And still
we are seeking our own Saviour.

Let us not deceive ourselves. A Jewish teacher of the
first century can never satisfy the longing of our souls.
Clothe Him with all the art of modern research, throw
upon Him the warm, deceptive calcium-light of modern
sentimentality; and despite it all common sense will come
to its rights again, and for our brief hour of self-decep-
tion—as though we had been with Jesus—will wreak upon
us the revenge of hopeless disillusionment.

But, says the modern preacher, are we not, in being
satisfied with the "historical" Jesus, the great teacher who
proclaimed the Kingdom of God, merely restoring the
simplicity of the primitive gospel? No, we answer, you
are not, but, temporally at least, you are not so very far
wrong. You are really returning to a very primitive

stage in the life of the Church. Only, that stage is not
the Galilean springtime. For in Galilee men had a living
Saviour. There was one time and one time only when the
disciples lived, like you, merely on the memory of Jesus.
When was it? It was a gloomy, desperate time. It was
the three sad days after the crucifixion. Then and then
only did Jesus' disciples regard Him merely as a blessed
memory. "We trusted," they said, "that it had been he
which should have redeemed Israel." "We trusted"—but
now our trust is gone. Shall we remain, with modern liberalism, forever in the gloom of those sad days? Or shall
we pass out from it to the warmth and joy of Pentecost?

Certainly we shall remain forever in the gloom if we
attend merely to the character of Jesus and neglect the
thing that He has done, if we try to attend to the Person
and neglect the message. We may have joy for sadness
and power for weakness; but not by easy half-way measures, not by avoidance of controversy, not by trying to
hold on to Jesus and yet reject the gospel. What was it
that within a few days transformed a band of mourners
into the spiritual conquerors of the world? It was not
the memory of Jesus' life; it was not the inspiration which
came from past contact with Him. But it was the message, "He is risen." That message alone gave to the disciples a living Saviour; and it alone can give to us a living
Saviour to-day. We shall never have vital contact with
Jesus if we attend to His person and neglect the message;
for it is the message which makes Him ours.

But the Christian message contains more than the fact
of the resurrection.[1] It is not enough to know that Jesus
is alive; it is not enough to know that a wonderful Person

[1] For what follows compare *A Rapid Survey of the History and
Literature of New Testament Times,* published by the Presbyterian
Board of Publication and Sabbath School Work, Teacher's Manual,
pp. 44f.

lived in the first century of the Christian era and that that
Person still lives, somewhere and somehow, to-day. Jesus
lives, and that is well; but what good is it to us? We are
like the inhabitants of far-off Syria or Phœnicia in the
days of His flesh. There is a wonderful Person who can
heal every ill of body and mind. But, alas, we are not
with Him, and the way is far. How shall we come into
His presence? How shall contact be established between
us and Him? For the people of ancient Galilee contact
was established by a touch of Jesus' hand or a word from
His lips. But for us the problem is not so easy. We
cannot find Him by the lake shore or in crowded houses;
we cannot be lowered into any room where He sits amid
scribes and Pharisees. If we employ only our own methods of search, we shall find ourselves on a fruitless pil-
grimage. Surely we need guidance, if we are to find our
Saviour.

And in the New Testament we find guidance full and
free—guidance so complete as to remove all doubt, yet
so simple that a child can understand. Contact with
Jesus according to the New Testament is established by
what Jesus does, not for others, but for us. The account
of what Jesus did for others is indeed necessary. By
reading how He went about doing good, how He healed
the sick and raised the dead and forgave sins, we learn
that He is a Person who is worthy of trust. But such
knowledge is to the Christian man not an end in itself,
but a means to an end. It is not enough to know that
Jesus is a Person worthy of trust; it is also necessary to
know that He is willing to have *us* trust Him. It is not
enough that He saved others; we need to know also that
He has saved us.

That knowledge is given in the story of the Cross. For
us Jesus does not merely place His fingers in the ears and

say, "Be opened"; for us He does not merely say "Arise and walk." For us He has done a greater thing—for us He died. Our dreadful guilt, the condemnation of God's law—it was wiped out by an act of grace. That is the message which brings Jesus near to us, and makes Him not merely the Saviour of the men of Galilee long ago, but the Saviour of you and me.

It is vain, then, to speak of reposing trust in the Person without believing the message. For trust involves a personal relation between the one who trusts and him in whom the trust is reposed. And in this case the personal relation is set up by the blessed theology of the Cross. Without the eighth chapter of Romans, the mere story of the earthly life of Jesus would be remote and dead; for it is through the eighth chapter of Romans, or the message which that chapter contains, that Jesus becomes our Saviour to-day.

The truth is that when men speak of trust in Jesus' Person, as being possible without acceptance of the message of His death and resurrection, they do not really mean trust at all. What they designate as trust is really admiration or reverence. They reverence Jesus as the supreme Person of all history and the supreme revealer of God. But trust can come only when the supreme Person extends His saving power *to us*. "He went about doing good," "He spake words such as never man spake," "He is the express image of God"—that is reverence; "He loved me and gave Himself for me"—that is faith.

But the words "He loved me and gave Himself for me" are in historical form; they constitute an account of something that happened. And they add to the fact the meaning of the fact; they contain in essence the whole profound theology of redemption through the blood of Christ. Christian doctrine lies at the very roots of faith.

It must be admitted, then, that if we are to have a non-doctrinal religion, or a doctrinal religion founded merely on general truth, we must give up not only Paul, not only the primitive Jerusalem Church, but also Jesus Himself. But what is meant by doctrine? It has been interpreted here as meaning any presentation of the facts which lie at the basis of the Christian religion with the true meaning of the facts. But is that the only sense of the word? May the word not also be taken in a narrower sense? May it not also mean a systematic and minute and one-sidedly scientific presentation of the facts? And if the word is taken in this narrower sense, may not the modern objection to doctrine involve merely an objection to the excessive subtlety of controversial theology, and not at all an objection to the glowing words of the New Testament, an objection to the sixteenth and seventeenth centuries and not at all to the first century? Undoubtedly the word is so taken by many occupants of the pews when they listen to the modern exaltation of "life" at the expense of "doctrine." The pious hearer labors under the impression that he is merely being asked to return to the simplicity of the New Testament, instead of attending to the subtleties of the theologians. Since it has never occurred to him to attend to the subtleties of the theologians, he has that comfortable feeling which always comes to the churchgoer when some one else's sins are being attacked. It is no wonder that the modern invectives against doctrine constitute a popular type of preaching. At any rate, an attack upon Calvin or Turrettin or the Westminster divines does not seem to the modern churchgoer to be a very dangerous thing. In point of fact, however, the attack upon doctrine is not nearly so innocent a matter as our simple churchgoer supposes; for the things objected to in the theology of the Church are also at the very heart of the New Testament. Ultimately the attack is not against the seventeenth century, but against the Bible and against Jesus Himself.

Even if it were an attack not upon the Bible but only upon the great historic presentations of Biblical teaching, it would still be unfortunate. If the Church were led to wipe out of existence all products of the thinking of nineteen Christian centuries and start fresh, the loss, even if the Bible were retained, would be immense. When it is once admitted that a body of facts lies at the basis of the Christian religion, the efforts which past generations have made toward the classification of the facts will have to be treated with respect. In no branch of science would there be any real advance if every generation started fresh with no dependence upon what past generations have achieved. Yet in theology, vituperation of the past seems to be thought essential to progress. And upon what base slanders the vituperation is based! After listening to modern tirades against the great creeds of the Church, one receives rather a shock when one turns to the Westminster Confession, for example, or to that tenderest and most theological of books, the "Pilgrim's Progress" of John Bunyan, and discovers that in doing so one has turned from shallow modern phrases to a "dead orthodoxy" that is pulsating with life in every word. In such orthodoxy there is life enough to set the whole world aglow with Christian love.

As a matter of fact, however, in the modern vituperation of "doctrine," it is not merely the great theologians or the great creeds that are being attacked, but the New Testament and our Lord Himself. In rejecting doctrine, the liberal preacher is rejecting the simple words of Paul, "Who loved me and gave Himself for me," just as much as the *homoousion* of the Nicene Creed. For the word "doctrine" is really used not in its narrowest, but in its broadest sense. The liberal preacher is really rejecting the whole basis of Christianity, which is a religion founded not on aspirations, but on facts. Here is found the most fundamental difference between liberalism and Christianity—liberalism is altogether in the imperative mood, while Christianity begins with a triumphant indicative; liberalism appeals to man's will, while Christianity announces, first, a gracious act of God.

In maintaining the doctrinal basis of Christianity, we are particularly anxious not to be misunderstood. There are certain things that we do not mean.

In the first place, we do not mean that if doctrine is sound it makes no difference about life. On the contrary, it makes all the difference in the world. From the beginning, Christianity was certainly a way of life; the salvation that it offered was a salvation from sin, and salvation from sin appeared not merely in a blessed hope but also in an immediate moral change. The early Christians, to the astonishment of their neighbors, lived a strange new kind of life—a life of honesty, of purity and of unselfishness. And from the Christian community all other types of life were excluded in the strictest way. From the beginning Christianity was certainly a life.

But how was the life produced? It might conceivably have been produced by exhortation. That method had often been tried in the ancient world; in the Hellenistic age there were many wandering preachers who told men how they ought to live. But such exhortation proved to be powerless. Although the ideals of the Cynic and Stoic preachers were high, these preachers never succeeded in transforming society. The strange thing about Christianity was that it adopted an entirely different method. It transformed the lives of men not by appealing to the

human will, but by telling a story; not by exhortation,
but by the narration of an event. It is no wonder that
such a method seemed strange. Could anything be more
impractical than the attempt to influence conduct by
rehearsing events concerning the death of a religious
teacher? That is what Paul called "the foolishness of the
message." It seemed foolish to the ancient world, and it
seems foolish to liberal preachers to-day. But the strange
thing is that it works. The effects of it appear even in
this world. Where the most eloquent exhortation fails,
the simple story of an event succeeds; the lives of men are
transformed by a piece of news.

It is especially by such transformation of life, to-day
as always, that the Christian message is commended to the
attention of men. Certainly, then, it does make an enormous difference whether our lives be right. If our doctrine be true, and our lives be wrong, how terrible is our
sin! For then we have brought despite upon the truth
itself. On the other hand, however, it is also very sad
when men use the social graces which God has given them,
and the moral momentum of a godly ancestry, to commend
a message which is false. Nothing in the world can take
the place of truth.

In the second place, we do not mean, in insisting upon
the doctrinal basis of Christianity, that all points of doctrine are equally important. It is perfectly possible for
Christian fellowship to be maintained despite differences
of opinion.

One such difference of opinion, which has been attaining
increasing prominence in recent years, concerns the order
of events in connection with the Lord's return. A large
number of Christian people believe that when evil has
reached its climax in the world, the Lord Jesus will return
to this earth in bodily presence to bring about a reign of

righteousness which will last a thousand years, and that only after that period the end of the world will come. That belief, in the opinion of the present writer, is an error, arrived at by a false interpretation of the Word of God; we do not think that the prophecies of the Bible permit so definite a mapping-out of future events. The Lord will come again, and it will be no mere "spiritual" coming in the modern sense—so much is clear—but that so little will be accomplished by the present dispensation of the Holy Spirit and so much will be left to be accomplished by the Lord in bodily presence—such a view we cannot find to be justified by the words of Scripture. What is our attitude, then, with regard to this debate? Certainly it cannot be an attitude of indifference. The recrudescence of "Chiliasm" or "premillennialism" in the modern Church causes us serious concern; it is coupled, we think, with a false method of interpreting Scripture which in the long run will be productive of harm. Yet how great is our agreement with those who hold the premillennial view! They share to the full our reverence for the authority of the Bible, and differ from us only in the interpretation of the Bible; they share our ascription of deity to the Lord Jesus, and our supernaturalistic conception both of the entrance of Jesus into the world and of the consummation when He shall come again. Certainly, then, from our point of view, their error, serious though it may be, is not deadly error; and Christian fellowship, with loyalty not only to the Bible but to the great creeds of the Church, can still unite us with them. It is therefore highly misleading when modern liberals represent the present issue in the Church, both in the mission field and at home, as being an issue between premillennialism and the opposite view. It is really an issue between Christianity, whether premillennial or not, on the one side, and a naturalistic negation of all Christianity on the other.

Another difference of opinion which can subsist in the midst of Christian fellowship is the difference of opinion about the mode of efficacy of the sacraments. That difference is indeed serious, and to deny its seriousness is a far greater error than to take the wrong side in the controversy itself. It is often said that the divided condition of Christendom is an evil, and so it is. But the evil consists in the existence of the errors which cause the divisions and not at all in the recognition of those errors when once they exist. It was a great calamity when at the "Marburg Conference" between Luther and the representatives of the Swiss Reformation, Luther wrote on the table with regard to the Lord's Supper, "This is my body," and said to Zwingli and Oecolampadius, "You have another spirit." That difference of opinion led to the breach between the Lutheran and the Reformed branches of the Church, and caused Protestantism to lose much of the ground that might otherwise have been gained. It was a great calamity indeed. But the calamity was due to the fact that Luther (as we believe) was wrong about the Lord's Supper; and it would have been a far greater calamity if being wrong about the Supper he had represented the whole question as a trifling affair. Luther was wrong about the Supper, but not nearly so wrong as he would have been if, being wrong, he had said to his opponents: "Brethren, this matter is a trifle; and it makes really very little difference what a man thinks about the table of the Lord." Such indifferentism would have been far more deadly than all the divisions between the branches of the Church. A Luther who would have compromised with regard to the Lord's Supper never would have said at the Diet of Worms, "Here I stand, I cannot do otherwise,

God help me, Amen." Indifferentism about doctrine makes no heroes of the faith.

Still another difference of opinion concerns the nature and prerogatives of the Christian ministry. According to Anglican doctrine, the bishops are in possession of an authority which has been handed down to them, by successive ordination, from the apostles of the Lord, and without such ordination there is no valid priesthood. Other churches deny this doctrine of "apostolic succession," and hold a different view of the ministry. Here again, the difference is no trifle, and we have little sympathy with those who in the mere interests of Church efficiency try to induce Anglicans to let down the barrier which their principles have led them to erect. But despite the importance of this difference, it does not descend to the very roots. Even to the conscientious Anglican himself, though he regards the members of other bodies as in schism, Christian fellowship with individuals in those other bodies is still possible; and certainly those who reject the Anglican view of the ministry can regard the Anglican Church as a genuine and very noble member in the body of Christ.

Another difference of opinion is that between the Calvinistic or Reformed theology and the Arminianism which appears in the Methodist Church. It is difficult to see how any one who has really studied the question can regard that difference as an unimportant matter. On the contrary, it touches very closely some of the profoundest things of the Christian faith. A Calvinist is constrained to regard the Arminian theology as a serious impoverishment of the Scripture doctrine of divine grace; and equally serious is the view which the Arminian must hold as to the doctrine of the Reformed Churches. Yet here again, true evangelical fellowship is possible between those who hold, with regard to some exceedingly important matters, sharply opposing views.

Far more serious still is the division between the Church of Rome and evangelical Protestantism in all its forms. Yet how great is the common heritage which unites the Roman Catholic Church, with its maintenance of the authority of Holy Scripture and with its acceptance of the great early creeds, to devout Protestants to-day! We would not indeed obscure the difference which divides us from Rome. The gulf is indeed profound. But profound as it is, it seems almost trifling compared to the abyss which stands between us and many ministers of our own Church. The Church of Rome may represent a perversion of the Christian religion; but naturalistic liberalism is not Christianity at all.

That does not mean that conservatives and liberals must live in personal animosity. It does not involve any lack of sympathy on our part for those who have felt obliged by the current of the times to relinquish their confidence in the strange message of the Cross. Many ties—ties of blood, of citizenship, of ethical aims, of humanitarian endeavor—unite us to those who have abandoned the gospel. We trust that those ties may never be weakened, and that ultimately they may serve some purpose in the propagation of the Christian faith. But Christian service consists primarily in the propagation of a message, and specifically Christian fellowship exists only between those to whom the message has become the very basis of all life.

The character of Christianity as founded upon a message is summed up in the words of the eighth verse of the first chapter of Acts—"Ye shall be my witnesses both in Jerusalem, and in all Judea and Samaria, and unto the uttermost part of the earth." It is entirely unnecessary,

for the present purpose, to argue about the historical
value of the Book of Acts or to discuss the question
whether Jesus really spoke the words just quoted. In
any case the verse must be recognized as an adequate
summary of what is known about primitive Christianity.
From the beginning Christianity was a campaign of witnessing. And the witnessing did not concern merely what
Jesus was doing within the recesses of the individual life.
To take the words of Acts in that way is to do violence
to the context and to all the evidence. On the contrary,
the Epistles of Paul and all the sources make it abundantly plain that the testimony was primarily not to inner
spiritual facts but to what Jesus had done once for all in
His death and resurrection.

Christianity is based, then, upon an account of something that happened, and the Christian worker is primarily a witness. But if so, it is rather important that
the Christian worker should tell the truth. When a man
takes his seat upon the witness stand, it makes little difference what the cut of his coat is, or whether his sen-
tences are nicely turned. The important thing is that he
tell the truth, the whole truth, and nothing but the truth.
If we are to be truly Christians, then, it does make a vast
difference what our teachings are, and it is by no means
aside from the point to set forth the teachings of Christianity in contrast with the teachings of the chief modern
rival of Christianity.

The chief modern rival of Christianity is "liberalism."
An examination of the teachings of liberalism in compari-
son with those of Christianity will show that at every
point the two movements are in direct opposition. That
examination will now be undertaken, though merely in a
summary and cursory way.

CHAPTER III

It has been observed in the last chapter that Christianity is based on an account of something that happened in the first century of our era. But before that account can be received, certain presuppositions must be accepted. The Christian gospel consists in an account of how God saved man, and before that gospel can be understood something must be known (1) about God and (2) about man. The doctrine of God and the doctrine of man are the two great presuppositions of the gospel. With regard to these presuppositions, as with regard to the gospel itself, modern liberalism is diametrically opposed to Christianity.

It is opposed to Christianity, in the first place, in its conception of God. But at this point we are met with a particularly insistent form of that objection to doctrinal matters which has already been considered. It is unnecessary, we are told, to have a "conception" of God; theology, or the knowledge of God, it is said, is the death of religion; we should not seek to know God, but should merely feel His presence.

With regard to this objection, it ought to be observed that if religion consists merely in feeling the presence of God, it is devoid of any moral quality whatever. Pure feeling, if there be such a thing, is non-moral. What makes affection for a human friend, for example, such an ennobling thing is the knowledge which we possess of the

54

character of our friend. Human affection, apparently so
simple, is really just bristling with dogma. It depends
upon a host of observations treasured up in the mind
with regard to the character of our friends. But if
human affection is thus really dependent upon knowledge,
why should it be otherwise with that supreme personal
relationship which is at the basis of religion? Why
should we be indignant about slanders directed against a
human friend, while at the same time we are patient about
the basest slanders directed against our God? Certainly
it does make the greatest possible difference what we
think about God; the knowledge of God is the very basis
of religion.

How, then, shall God be known; how shall we become
so acquainted with Him that personal fellowship may
become possible? Some liberal preachers would say that
we become acquainted with God only through Jesus.
That assertion has an appearance of loyalty to our Lord,
but in reality it is highly derogatory to Him. For Jesus
Himself plainly recognized the validity of other ways of
knowing God, and to reject those other ways is to reject
the things that lay at the very centre of Jesus' life. Jesus
plainly found God's hand in nature; the lilies of the field
revealed to Him the weaving of God. He found God also
in the moral law; the law written in the hearts of men was
God's law, which revealed His righteousness. Finally
Jesus plainly found God revealed in the Scriptures. How
profound was our Lord's use of the words of prophets and
psalmists! To say that such revelation of God was in-
valid, or is useless to us to-day, is to do despite to things
that lay closest to Jesus' mind and heart.

But, as a matter of fact, when men say that we know
God only as He is revealed in Jesus, they are denying all
real knowledge of God whatever. For unless there be

some idea of God independent of Jesus, the ascription of deity to Jesus has no meaning. To say, "Jesus is God," is meaningless unless the word "God" has an antecedent meaning attached to it. And the attaching of a meaning to the word "God" is accomplished by the means which have just been mentioned. We are not forgetting the words of Jesus in the Gospel of John, "He that hath seen me hath seen the Father." But these words do not mean that if a man had never known what the word "God" means, he could come to attach an idea to that word merely by his knowledge of Jesus' character. On the contrary, the disciples to whom Jesus was speaking had already a very definite conception of God; a knowledge of the one supreme Person was presupposed in all that Jesus said. But the disciples desired not only a knowledge of God but also intimate, personal contact. And that came through their intercourse with Jesus. Jesus revealed, in a wonderfully intimate way, the character of God, but such revelation obtained its true significance only on the basis both of the Old Testament heritage and of Jesus' own teaching. Rational theism, the knowledge of one Supreme Person, Maker and active Ruler of the world, is at the very root of Christianity.

But, the modern preacher will say, it is incongruous to attribute to Jesus an acceptance of "rational theism"; Jesus had a practical, not a theoretical, knowledge of God. There is a sense in which these words are true. Certainly no part of Jesus' knowledge of God was merely theoretical; everything that Jesus knew about God touched His heart and determined His actions. In that sense, Jesus' knowledge of God was "practical." But unfortunately that is not the sense in which the assertion of modern liberalism is meant. What is frequently meant by a "practical" knowledge of God in modern parlance is not a theoretical knowledge of God that is also practical, but a practical knowledge which is not theoretical —in other words, a knowledge which gives no information about objective reality, a knowledge which is no knowledge at all. And nothing could possibly be more unlike the religion of Jesus than that. The relation of Jesus to His heavenly Father was not a relation to a vague and impersonal goodness, it was not a relation which merely clothed itself in symbolic, personal form. On the contrary, it was a relation to a real Person, whose existence was just as definite and just as much a subject of theoretic knowledge as the existence of the lilies of the field that God had clothed. The very basis of the religion of Jesus was a triumphant belief in the real existence of a personal God.

And without that belief no type of religion can rightly appeal to Jesus to-day. Jesus was a theist, and rational theism is at the basis of Christianity. Jesus did not, indeed, support His theism by argument; He did not provide in advance answers to the Kantian attack upon the theistic proofs. But that means not that He was indifferent to the belief which is the logical result of those proofs, but that the belief stood so firm, both to Him and to His hearers, that in His teaching it is always presupposed. So to-day it is not necessary for all Christians to analyze the logical basis of their belief in God; the human mind has a wonderful faculty for the condensation of perfectly valid arguments, and what seems like an instinctive belief may turn out to be the result of many logical steps. Or, rather, it may be that the belief in a personal God is the result of a primitive revelation, and that the theistic proofs are only the logical confirmation of what was originally arrived at by a different means. At any rate, the logical confirmation of the belief in God is a vital concern

to the Christian; at this point as at many others religion
and philosophy are connected in the most intimate possible way. True religion can make no peace with a false
philosophy, any more than with a science that is falsely
so-called; a thing cannot possibly be true in religion and
false in philosophy or in science. All methods of arriving
at truth, if they be valid methods, will arrive at a harmonious result. Certainly the atheistic or agnostic Christianity which sometimes goes under the name of a "practical" religion is no Christianity at all. At the very root of
Christianity is the belief in the real existence of a personal
God.

Strangely enough, at the very time when modern liberalism is decrying the theistic proofs, and taking refuge
in a "practical" knowledge which shall somehow be independent of scientifically or philosophically ascertained
facts, the liberal preacher loves to use one designation of
God which is nothing if not theistic; he loves to speak of
God as "Father." The term certainly has the merit of
ascribing personality to God. By some of those who use
it, indeed, it is not seriously meant; by some it is employed because it is useful, not because it is true. But
not all liberals are able to make the subtle distinction
between theoretic judgments and judgments of value;
some liberals, though perhaps a decreasing number, are
true believers in a personal God. And such men are able
to think of God truly as a Father.

The term presents a very lofty conception of God. It
is not indeed exclusively Christian; the term "Father" has
been applied to God outside of Christianity. It appears,
for example, in the widespread belief in an "All-Father,"
which prevails among many races even in company with
polytheism; it appears here and there in the Old Testament, and in pre-Christian Jewish writings subsequent to

the Old Testament period. Such occurrences of the term are by no means devoid of significance. The Old Testament usage, in particular, is a worthy precursor of our Lord's teaching; for although in the Old Testament the word "Father" ordinarily designates God in relation not to the individual, but to the nation or to the king, yet the individual Israelite, because of his part in the chosen people, felt himself to be in a peculiarly intimate relation to the covenant God. But despite this anticipation of the teaching of our Lord, Jesus brought such an incomparable enrichment of the usage of the term, that it is a correct instinct which regards the thought of God as Father as something characteristically Christian.

Modern men have been so much impressed with this element in Jesus' teaching that they have sometimes been inclined to regard it as the very sum and substance of our religion. We are not interested, they say, in many things for which men formerly gave their lives; we are not interested in the theology of the creeds; we are not interested in the doctrines of sin and salvation; we are not interested in atonement through the blood of Christ: enough for us is the simple truth of the fatherhood of God and its corollary, the brotherhood of man. We may not be very orthodox in the theological sense, they continue, but of course you will recognize us as Christians because we accept Jesus' teaching as to the Father God.

It is very strange how intelligent persons can speak in this way. It is very strange how those who accept only the universal fatherhood of God as the sum and substance of religion can regard themselves as Christians or can appeal to Jesus of Nazareth. For the plain fact is that this modern doctrine of the universal fatherhood of God formed no part whatever of Jesus' teaching. Where is it that Jesus may be supposed to have taught the universal

fatherhood of God? Certainly it is not in the parable of
the Prodigal Son. For in the first place, the publicans
and sinners whose acceptance by Jesus formed the occasion both of the Pharisees' objection and of Jesus' answer
to them by means of the parable, were not any men any-
where, but were members of the chosen people and as such
might be designated as sons of God. In the second place,
a parable is certainly not to be pressed in its details. So
here because the joy of the father in the parable is like
the joy of God when a sinner receives salvation at Jesus'
hand, it does not follow that the relation which God sustains to still unrepentant sinners is that of a Father to his
children. Where else, then, can the universal fatherhood
of God be found? Surely not in the Sermon on the
Mount; for throughout the Sermon on the Mount those
who can call God Father are distinguished in the most
emphatic way from the great world of the Gentiles outside. One passage in the discourse has indeed been urged
in support of the modern doctrine: "But I say unto you,
love your enemies and pray for them that persecute you;
that ye may be sons of your Father who is in heaven; for
He maketh His sun to rise on evil and good and sendeth
rain on just and unjust" (Matt. v. 44, 45). But the
passage certainly will not bear the weight which is hung
upon it. God is indeed represented here as caring for all
men whether evil or good, but He is certainly not called
the Father of all. Indeed it might almost be said that the
point of the passage depends on the fact that He is not
the Father of all. He cares even for those who are not
His children but His enemies; so His children, Jesus' disciples, ought to imitate Him by loving even those who are
not their brethren but their persecutors. The modern
doctrine of the universal fatherhood of God is not to be
found in the teaching of Jesus.

And it is not to be found in the New Testament. The whole New Testament and Jesus Himself do indeed represent God as standing in a relation to all men, whether Christians or not, which is analogous to that in which a father stands to his children. He is the Author of the being of all, and as such might well be called the Father of all. He cares for all, and for that reason also might be called the Father of all. Here and there the figure of fatherhood seems to be used to designate this broader relationship which God sustains to all men or even to all created beings. So in an isolated passage in Hebrews, God is spoken of as the "Father of spirits" (Heb. xii. 9). Here perhaps it is the relation of God, as creator, to the personal beings whom He has created which is in view. One of the clearest instances of the broader use of the figure of fatherhood is found in the speech of Paul at Athens, Acts xvii. 28: "For we are also His offspring." Here it is plainly the relation in which God stands to all men, whether Christians or not, which is in mind. But the words form part of an hexameter line and are taken from a pagan poet; they are not represented as part of the gospel, but merely as belonging to the common meeting-ground which Paul discovered in speaking to his pagan hearers. This passage is only typical of what appears, with respect to a universal fatherhood of God, in the New Testament as a whole. Something analogous to a universal fatherhood of God is taught in the New Testament. Here and there the terminology of fatherhood and sonship is even used to describe this general relationship. But such instances are extremely rare. Ordinarily the lofty term "Father" is used to describe a relationship of a far more intimate kind, the relationship in which God stands to the company of the redeemed.

The modern doctrine of the universal fatherhood of

God, then, which is being celebrated as "the essence of Christianity," really belongs at best only to that vague natural religion which forms the presupposition which the Christian preacher can use when the gospel is to be proclaimed; and when it is regarded as a reassuring, all-sufficient thing, it comes into direct opposition to the New Testament. The gospel itself refers to something entirely different; the really distinctive New Testament teaching about the fatherhood of God concerns only those who have been brought into the household of faith.

There is nothing narrow about such teaching; for the door of the household of faith is open wide to all. That door is the "new and living way" which Jesus opened by His blood. And if we really love our fellowmen, we shall not go about the world, with the liberal preacher, trying to make men satisfied with the coldness of a vague natural religion. But by the preaching of the gospel we shall invite them into the warmth and joy of the house of God. Christianity offers men all that is offered by the modern liberal teaching about the universal fatherhood of God; but it is Christianity only because it offers also infinitely more.

But the liberal conception of God differs even more fundamentally from the Christian view than in the different circle of ideas connected with the terminology of fatherhood. The truth is that liberalism has lost sight of the very centre and core of the Christian teaching. In the Christian view of God as set forth in the Bible, there are many elements. But one attribute of God is absolutely fundamental in the Bible; one attribute is absolutely necessary in order to render intelligible all the rest. That attribute is the awful transcendence of God. From beginning to end the Bible is concerned to set forth the awful gulf that separates the creature from the Creator. It is true, indeed, that according to the Bible God is immanent in the world. Not a sparrow falls to the ground without Him. But he is immanent in the world not because He is identified with the world, but because He is the free Creator and Upholder of it. Between the creature and the Creator a great gulf is fixed.

In modern liberalism, on the other hand, this sharp distinction between God and the world is broken down, and the name "God" is applied to the mighty world process itself. We find ourselves in the midst of a mighty process, which manifests itself in the indefinitely small and in the indefinitely great—in the infinitesimal life which is revealed through the microscope and in the vast movements of the heavenly spheres. To this world-process, of which we ourselves form a part, we apply the dread name of "God." God, therefore, it is said in effect, is not a person distinct from ourselves; on the contrary our life is a part of His. Thus the Gospel story of the Incarnation, according to modern liberalism, is sometimes thought of as a symbol of the general truth that man at his best is one with God.

It is strange how such a representation can be regarded as anything new, for as a matter of fact, pantheism is a very ancient phenomenon. It has always been with us, to blight the religious life of man. And modern liberalism, even when it is not consistently pantheistic, is at any rate pantheizing. It tends everywhere to break down the separateness between God and the world, and the sharp personal distinction between God and man. Even the sin of man on this view ought logically to be regarded as part of the life of God. Very different is the living and holy God of the Bible and of Christian faith.

Christianity differs from liberalism, then, in the first place, in its conception of God. But it also differs in its conception of man.

Modern liberalism has lost all sense of the gulf that
separates the creature from the Creator; its doctrine of
man follows naturally from its doctrine of God. But it
is not only the creature limitations of mankind which are
denied. Even more important is another difference. According to the Bible, man is a sinner under the just condemnation of God; according to modern liberalism, there
is really no such thing as sin. At the very root of the
modern liberal movement is the loss of the consciousness
of sin.[1]

The consciousness of sin was formerly the starting-
point of all preaching; but to-day it is gone. Characteristic of the modern age, above all else, is a supreme
confidence in human goodness; the religious literature of
the day is redolent of that confidence. Get beneath the
rough exterior of men, we are told, and we shall discover
enough self-sacrifice to found upon it the hope of society;
the world's evil, it is said, can be overcome with the
world's good; no help is needed from outside the world.

What has produced this satisfaction with human goodness? What has become of the consciousness of sin? The
consciousness of sin has certainly been lost. But what has
removed it from the hearts of men?

In the first place, the war has perhaps had something
to do with the change. In time of war, our attention is
called so exclusively to the sins of other people that we
are sometimes inclined to forget our own sins. Attention
to the sins of other people is, indeed, sometimes necessary.
It is quite right to be indignant against any oppression of
the weak which is being carried on by the strong. But
such a habit of mind, if made permanent, if carried over
into the days of peace, has its dangers. It joins forces

[1] For what follows, see "The Church in the War," in *The Presbyterian*, for May 29, 1919, pp. 10f.

with the collectivism of the modern state to obscure the individual, personal character of guilt. If John Smith beats his wife nowadays, no one is so old-fashioned as to blame John Smith for it. On the contrary, it is said, John Smith is evidently the victim of some more of that Bolshevistic propaganda; Congress ought to be called in extra session in order to take up the case of John Smith in an alien and sedition law.

But the loss of the consciousness of sin is far deeper than the war; it has its roots in a mighty spiritual process which has been active during the past seventy-five years. Like other great movements, that process has come silently—so silently that its results have been achieved before the plain man was even aware of what was taking place. Nevertheless, despite all superficial continuity, a remarkable change has come about within the last seventy-five years. The change is nothing less than the substitution of paganism for Christianity as the dominant view of life. Seventy-five years ago, Western civilization, despite inconsistencies, was still predominantly Christian; to-day it is predominantly pagan.

In speaking of "paganism," we are not using a term of reproach. Ancient Greece was pagan, but it was glorious, and the modern world has not even begun to equal its achievements. What, then, is paganism? The answer is not really difficult. Paganism is that view of life which finds the highest goal of human existence in the healthy and harmonious and joyous development of existing human faculties. Very different is the Christian ideal. Paganism is optimistic with regard to unaided human nature, whereas Christianity is the religion of the broken heart.

In saying that Christianity is the religion of the broken heart, we do not mean that Christianity ends with the

broken heart; we do not mean that the characteristic
Christian attitude is a continual beating on the breast or
a continual crying of "Woe is me." Nothing could be
further from the fact. On the contrary, Christianity
means that sin is faced once for all, and then is cast, by
the grace of God, forever into the depths of the sea. The
trouble with the paganism of ancient Greece, as with the
paganism of modern times, was not in the superstruc-
ture, which was glorious, but in the foundation, which was
rotten. There was always something to be covered up;
the enthusiasm of the architect was maintained only by
ignoring the disturbing fact of sin. In Christianity, on
the other hand, nothing needs to be covered up. The
fact of sin is faced squarely once for all, and is dealt with
by the grace of God. But then, after sin has been removed
by the grace of God, the Christian can proceed to develop
joyously every faculty that God has given him. Such is
the higher Christian humanism—a humanism founded not
upon human pride but upon divine grace.

But although Christianity does not end with the broken
heart, it does begin with the broken heart; it begins with
the consciousness of sin. Without the consciousness of
sin, the whole of the gospel will seem to be an idle tale.
But how can the consciousness of sin be revived? Something no doubt can be accomplished by the proclamation
of the law of God, for the law reveals transgressions. The
whole of the law, moreover, should be proclaimed. It will
hardly be wise to adopt the suggestion (recently offered
among many suggestions as to the ways in which we shall
have to modify our message in order to retain the alle-
giance of the returning soldiers) that we must stop treat-
ing the little sins as though they were big sins. That
suggestion means apparently that we must not worry too
much about the little sins, but must let them remain unmo-

lested. With regard to such an expedient, it may perhaps be suggested that in the moral battle we are fighting against a very resourceful enemy, who does not reveal the position of his guns by desultory artillery action when he plans a great attack. In the moral battle, as in the Great European War, the quiet sectors are usually the most dangerous. It is through the "little sins" that Satan gains an entrance into our lives. Probably, therefore, it will be prudent to watch all sectors of the front and lose no time about introducing the unity of command.

But if the consciousness of sin is to be produced, the law of God must be proclaimed in the lives of Christian people as well as in word. It is quite useless for the preacher to breathe out fire and brimstone from the pulpit, if at the same time the occupants of the pews go on taking sin very lightly and being content with the moral standards of the world. The rank and file of the Church must do their part in so proclaiming the law of God by their lives that the secrets of men's hearts shall be revealed.

All these things, however, are in themselves quite insufficient to produce the consciousness of sin. The more one observes the condition of the Church, the more one feels obliged to confess that the conviction of sin is a great mystery, which can be produced only by the Spirit of God. Proclamation of the law, in word and in deed, can prepare for the experience, but the experience itself comes from God. When a man has that experience, when a man comes under the conviction of sin, his whole attitude toward life is transformed; he wonders at his former blindness, and the message of the gospel, which formerly seemed to be an idle tale, becomes now instinct with light. But it is God alone who can produce the change.

Only, let us not try to do without the Spirit of God.

The fundamental fault of the modern Church is that she is busily engaged in an absolutely impossible task—she is busily engaged in calling the righteous to repentance. Modern preachers are trying to bring men into the Church without requiring them to relinquish their pride; they are trying to help men avoid the conviction of sin. The preacher gets up into the pulpit, opens the Bible, and addresses the congregation somewhat as follows: "You people are very good," he says; "you respond to every appeal that looks toward the welfare of the community. Now we have in the Bible—especially in the life of Jesus—something so good that we believe it is good enough even for you good people." Such is modern preaching. It is heard every Sunday in thousands of pulpits. But it is entirely futile. Even our Lord did not call the righteous to repentance, and probably we shall be no more successful than He.

CHAPTER IV

Modern liberalism, it has been observed so far, has lost sight of the two great presuppositions of the Christian message—the living God, and the fact of sin. The liberal doctrine of God and the liberal doctrine of man are both diametrically opposite to the Christian view. But the divergence concerns not only the presuppositions of the message, but also the message itself.

The Christian message has come to us through the Bible. What shall we think about this Book in which the message is contained?

According to the Christian view, the Bible contains an account of a revelation from God to man, which is found nowhere else. It is true, the Bible also contains a confirmation and a wonderful enrichment of the revelations which are given also by the things that God has made and by the conscience of man. "The heavens declare the glory of God; and the firmament showeth his handywork"— these words are a confirmation of the revelation of God in nature; "all have sinned and fall short of the glory of God"—these words are a confirmation of what is attested by the conscience. But in addition to such reaffirmations of what might conceivably be learned elsewhere—as a matter of fact, because of men's blindness, even so much is learned elsewhere only in comparatively obscure fashion— the Bible also contains an account of a revelation which is absolutely new. That new revelation concerns the way

69

by which sinful man can come into communion with the
living God.

The way was opened, according to the Bible, by an act
of God, when, almost nineteen hundred years ago, outside
the walls of Jerusalem, the eternal Son was offered as a
sacrifice for the sins of men. To that one great event the
whole Old Testament looks forward, and in that one event
the whole of the New Testament finds its centre and core.
Salvation then, according to the Bible, is not something
that was discovered, but something that happened. Hence
appears the uniqueness of the Bible. All the ideas of
Christianity might be discovered in some other religion,
yet there would be in that other religion no Christianity.
For Christianity depends, not upon a complex of ideas,
but upon the narration of an event. Without that event,
the world, in the Christian view, is altogether dark, and
humanity is lost under the guilt of sin. There can be no
salvation by the discovery of eternal truth, for eternal
truth brings naught but despair, because of sin. But a
new face has been put upon life by the blessed thing that
God did when He offered up His only begotten Son.

An objection is sometimes offered against this view of
the contents of the Bible.[1] Must we, it is said, depend
upon what happened so long ago? Does salvation wait
upon the examination of musty records? Is the trained
student of Palestinian history the modern priest without
whose gracious intervention no one can see God? Can we
not find, instead, a salvation that is independent of history, a salvation that depends only on what is with us
here and now?

The objection is not devoid of weight. But it ignores
one of the primary evidences for the truth of the gospel
record. That evidence is found in Christian experience.

[1] For what follows compare *History and Faith*, 1915, pp. 13-15.

Salvation does depend upon what happened long ago, but the event of long ago has effects that continue until to-day. We are told in the New Testament that Jesus offered Himself as a sacrifice for the sins of those who should believe on Him. That is a record of a past event. But we can make trial of it to-day, and making trial of it we find it to be true. We are told in the New Testament that on a certain morning long ago Jesus rose from the dead. That again is a record of a past event. But again we can make trial of it, and making trial of it we discover that Jesus is truly a living Saviour to-day.

But at this point a fatal error lies in wait. It is one of the root errors of modern liberalism. Christian experience, we have just said, is useful as confirming the gospel message. But because it is necessary, many men have jumped to the conclusion that it is all that is necessary. Having a present experience of Christ in the heart, may we not, it is said, hold that experience no matter what history may tell us as to the events of the first Easter morning? May we not make ourselves altogether independent of the results of Biblical criticism? No matter what sort of man history may tell us Jesus of Nazareth actually was, no matter what history may say about the real meaning of His death or about the story of His alleged resurrection, may we not continue to experience the presence of Christ in our souls?

The trouble is that the experience thus maintained is not Christian experience. Religious experience it may be, but Christian experience it certainly is not. For Christian experience depends absolutely upon an event. The Christian says to himself: "I have meditated upon the problem of becoming right with God, I have tried to produce a righteousness that will stand in His sight; but when I heard the gospel message I learned that what I had

weakly striven to accomplish had been accomplished by
the Lord Jesus Christ when He died for me on the Cross
and completed His redeeming work by the glorious resurrection. If the thing has not yet been done, if I merely
have an idea of its accomplishment, then I am of all men
most miserable, for I am still in my sins. My Christian
life, then, depends altogether upon the truth of the New
Testament record."

Christian experience is rightly used when it confirms the
documentary evidence. But it can never possibly provide
a substitute for the documentary evidence. We know that
the gospel story is true partly because of the early date
of the documents in which it appears, the evidence as to
their authorship, the internal evidence of their truth, the
impossibility of explaining them as being based upon de-
ception or upon myth. This evidence is gloriously confirmed by present experience, which adds to the documentary evidence that wonderful directness and immediacy
of conviction which delivers us from fear. Christian experience is rightly used when it helps to convince us that the
events narrated in the New Testament actually did occur;
but it can never enable us to be Christians whether the
events occurred or not. It is a fair flower, and should be
prized as a gift of God. But cut it from its root in the
blessed Book, and it soon withers away and dies.

Thus the revelation of which an account is contained in
the Bible embraces not only a reaffirmation of eternal
truths—itself necessary because the truths have been
obscured by the blinding effect of sin—but also a revelation which sets forth the meaning of an act of God.

The contents of the Bible, then, are unique. But
another fact about the Bible is also important. The Bible
might contain an account of a true revelation from God,
and yet the account be full of error. Before the full

authority of the Bible can be established, therefore, it is necessary to add to the Christian doctrine of revelation the Christian doctrine of inspiration. The latter doctrine means that the Bible not only is an account of important things, but that the account itself is true, the writers having been so preserved from error, despite a full maintenance of their habits of thought and expression, that the resulting Book is the "infallible rule of faith and practice."

This doctrine of "plenary inspiration" has been made the subject of persistent misrepresentation. Its opponents speak of it as though it involved a mechanical theory of the activity of the Holy Spirit. The Spirit, it is said, is represented in this doctrine as dictating the Bible to writers who were really little more than stenographers. But of course all such caricatures are without basis in fact, and it is rather surprising that intelligent men should be so blinded by prejudice about this matter as not even to examine for themselves the perfectly accessible treatises in which the doctrine of plenary inspiration is set forth. It is usually considered good practice to examine a thing for one's self before echoing the vulgar ridicule of it. But in connection with the Bible, such scholarly restraints are somehow regarded as out of place. It is so much easier to content one's self with a few opprobrious adjectives such as "mechanical," or the like. Why engage in serious criticism when the people prefer ridicule? Why attack a real opponent when it is easier to knock down a man of straw? [1]

---

[1] It is not denied that there are some persons in the modern Church who do neglect the context of Bible quotations and who do ignore the human characteristics of the Biblical writers. But in an entirely unwarrantable manner this defective way of using the Bible is attributed, by insinuation at least, to the great body of those who have held to the inspiration of Scripture.

As a matter of fact, the doctrine of plenary inspiration does not deny the individuality of the Biblical writers; it does not ignore their use of ordinary means for acquiring information; it does not involve any lack of interest in the historical situations which gave rise to the Biblical books. What it does deny is the presence of error in the Bible. It supposes that the Holy Spirit so informed the minds of the Biblical writers that they were kept from falling into the errors that mar all other books. The Bible might contain an account of a genuine revelation of God, and yet not contain a true account. But according to the doctrine of inspiration, the account is as a matter of fact a true account; the Bible is an "infallible rule of faith and practice."

Certainly that is a stupendous claim, and it is no wonder that it has been attacked. But the trouble is that the attack is not always fair. If the liberal preacher objected to the doctrine of plenary inspiration on the ground that as a matter of fact there are errors in the Bible, he might be right and he might be wrong, but at any rate the discussion would be conducted on the proper ground. But too often the preacher desires to avoid the delicate question of errors in the Bible—a question which might give offence to the rank and file—and prefers to speak merely against "mechanical" theories of inspiration, the theory of "dictation," the "superstitious use of the Bible as a talisman," or the like. It all sounds to the plain man as though it were very harmless. Does not the liberal preacher say that the Bible is "divine"—indeed that it is the more divine because it is the more human? What could be more edifying than that? But of course such appearances are deceptive. A Bible that is full of error is certainly divine in the modern pantheizing sense of "divine," according to which God is just another name for the course of the world with all its imperfections and all its sin. But the God whom the Christian worships is a God of truth. It must be admitted that there are many Christians who do not accept the doctrine of plenary inspiration. That doctrine is denied not only by liberal opponents of Christianity, but also by many true Christian men. There are many Christian men in the modern Church who find in the origin of Christianity no mere product of evolution but a real entrance of the creative power of God, who depend for their salvation, not at all upon their own efforts to lead the Christ life, but upon the atoning blood of Christ —there are many men in the modern Church who thus accept the central message of the Bible and yet believe that the message has come to us merely on the authority of trustworthy witnesses unaided in their literary work by any supernatural guidance of the Spirit of God. There are many who believe that the Bible is right at the central point, in its account of the redeeming work of Christ, and yet believe that it contains many errors. Such men are not really liberals, but Christians; because they have accepted as true the message upon which Christianity depends. A great gulf separates them from those who reject the supernatural act of God with which Christianity stands or falls.

It is another question, however, whether the mediating view of the Bible which is thus maintained is logically tenable, the trouble being that our Lord Himself seems to have held the high view of the Bible which is here being rejected. Certainly it is another question—and a question which the present writer would answer with an emphatic negative—whether the panic about the Bible, which gives rise to such concessions, is at all justified by the facts. If the Christian make full use of his Christian privileges, he finds the seat of authority in the whole

Bible, which he regards as no mere word of man but as
the very Word of God.

Very different is the view of modern liberalism. The
modern liberal rejects not only the doctrine of plenary
inspiration, but even such respect for the Bible as would
be proper over against any ordinarily trustworthy book.
But what is substituted for the Christian view of the
Bible? What is the liberal view as to the seat of authority
in religion? [1]

The impression is sometimes produced that the modern
liberal substitutes for the authority of the Bible the
authority of Christ. He cannot accept, he says, what he
regards as the perverse moral teaching of the Old Testament or the sophistical arguments of Paul. But he
regards himself as being the true Christian because,
rejecting the rest of the Bible, he depends upon Jesus
alone.

This impression, however, is utterly false. The modern
liberal does not really hold to the authority of Jesus.
Even if he did so, indeed, he would still be impoverishing
greatly his knowledge of God and of the way of salvation.
The words of Jesus, spoken during His earthly ministry,
could hardly contain all that we need to know about God
and about the way of salvation; for the meaning of Jesus'
redeeming work could hardly be fully set forth before that
work was done. It could be set forth indeed by way of
prophecy, and as a matter of fact it was so set forth by
Jesus even in the days of His flesh. But the full explanation could naturally be given only after the work was
done. And such was actually the divine method. It is
doing despite, not only to the Spirit of God, but also to
Jesus Himself, to regard the teaching of the Holy Spirit,

[1] For what follows, compare "For Christ or Against Him," in *The
Presbyterian,* for January 20, 1921, p. 9.

given through the apostles, as at all inferior in authority
to the teaching of Jesus. As a matter of fact, however, the modern liberal does
not hold fast even to the authority of Jesus. Certainly
he does not accept the words of Jesus as they are recorded
in the Gospels. For among the recorded words of Jesus
are to be found just those things which are most abhor-
rent to the modern liberal Church, and in His recorded
words Jesus also points forward to the fuller revelation
which was afterwards to be given through His apostles.
Evidently, therefore, those words of Jesus which are to
be regarded as authoritative by modern liberalism must
first be selected from the mass of the recorded words by a
critical process. The critical process is certainly very
difficult, and the suspicion often arises that the critic is
retaining as genuine words of the historical Jesus only
those words which conform to his own preconceived ideas.
But even after the sifting process has been completed, the
liberal scholar is still unable to accept as authoritative
all the sayings of Jesus; he must finally admit that even
the "historical" Jesus as reconstructed by modern historians said some things that are untrue.

So much is usually admitted. But, it is maintained,
although not everything that Jesus said is true, His central "life-purpose" is still to be regarded as regulative for
the Church. But what then was the life-purpose of Jesus?
According to the shortest, and if modern criticism be
accepted, the earliest of the Gospels, the Son of Man
"came not to be ministered unto, but to minister, and to
give his life a ransom for many" (Mark x. 45). Here the
vicarious death is put as the "life-purpose" of Jesus.
Such an utterance must of course be pushed aside by the
modern liberal Church. The truth is that the life-purpose
of Jesus discovered by modern liberalism is not the life-

purpose of the real Jesus, but merely represents those elements in the teaching of Jesus—isolated and misinter-
preted—which happen to agree with the modern program.
It is not Jesus, then, who is the real authority, but the
modern principle by which the selection within Jesus' recorded teaching has been made. Certain isolated ethical
principles of the Sermon on the Mount are accepted, not
at all because they are teachings of Jesus, but because
they agree with modern ideas.

It is not true at all, then, that modern liberalism is
based upon the authority of Jesus. It is obliged to reject
a vast deal that is absolutely essential in Jesus' example
and teaching—notably His consciousness of being the
heavenly Messiah. The real authority, for liberalism, can
only be "the Christian consciousness" or "Christian experience." But how shall the findings of the Christian consciousness be established? Surely not by a majority vote
of the organized Church. Such a method would obviously
do away with all liberty of conscience. The only authority, then, can be individual experience; truth can only be
that which "helps" the individual man. Such an authority
is obviously no authority at all; for individual experience
is endlessly diverse, and when once truth is regarded only
as that which works at any particular time, it ceases to
be truth. The result is an abysmal skepticism.

The Christian man, on the other hand, finds in the Bible
the very Word of God. Let it not be said that dependence
upon a book is a dead or an artificial thing. The Reformation of the sixteenth century was founded upon the
authority of the Bible, yet it set the world aflame.
Dependence upon a word of man would be slavish, but
dependence upon God's word is life. Dark and gloomy
would be the world, if we were left to our own devices, and
had no blessed Word of God. The Bible, to the Christian

is not a burdensome law, but the very Magna Charta of Christian liberty.

It is no wonder, then, that liberalism is totally different from Christianity, for the foundation is different. Christianity is founded upon the Bible. It bases upon the Bible both its thinking and its life. Liberalism on the other hand is founded upon the shifting emotions of sinful men.

CHAPTER V

Three points of difference between liberalism and Christianity have been noticed so far. The two religions are different with regard to the presuppositions of the Christian message, the view of God and the view of man; and they are also different with regard to their estimate of the Book in which the message is contained. It is not surprising, then, that they differ fundamentally with regard to the message itself. But before the message is considered, we must consider the Person upon whom the message is based. The Person is Jesus. And in their attitude toward Jesus, liberalism and Christianity are sharply opposed.

The Christian attitude toward Jesus appears in the whole New Testament. In examining the New Testament witness it has become customary in recent years to begin with the Epistles of Paul.[1] This custom is sometimes based upon error; it is sometimes based upon the view that the Epistles of Paul are "primary" sources of information, while the Gospels are considered to be only "secondary." As a matter of fact, the Gospels, as well as the Epistles, are primary sources of the highest possible value. But the custom of beginning with Paul is at least convenient. Its convenience is due to the large measure of agreement which prevails with regard to the Pauline Epis-

[1] This method of approach has been followed by the present writer in *The Origin of Paul's Religion,* 1921.

tles. About the date and authorship of the Gospels there is debate; but with regard to the authorship and approximate date of the principal epistles of Paul all serious historians, whether Christian or non-Christian, are agreed. It is universally admitted that the chief of the extant epistles attributed to Paul were really written by a man of the first Christian generation, who was himself a contemporary of Jesus and had come into personal contact with certain of Jesus' intimate friends. What, then, was the attitude of this representative of the first Christian generation toward Jesus of Nazareth?

The answer cannot be at all in doubt. The apostle Paul clearly stood always toward Jesus in a truly religious relationship. Jesus was not for Paul merely an example for faith; He was primarily the object of faith. The religion of Paul did not consist in having faith in God like the faith which Jesus had in God; it consisted rather in having faith in Jesus. An appeal to the example of Jesus is not indeed absent from the Pauline Epistles, and certainly it was not absent from Paul's life. The example of Jesus was found by Paul, moreover, not merely in the acts of incarnation and atonement but even in the daily life of Jesus in Palestine. Exaggeration with regard to this matter should be avoided. Plainly Paul knew far more about the life of Jesus than in the Epistles he has seen fit to tell; plainly the Epistles do not begin to contain all the instruction which Paul had given to the Churches at the commencement of their Christian life. But even after exaggerations have been avoided, the fact is significant enough. The plain fact is that imitation of Jesus, important though it was for Paul, was swallowed up by something far more important still. Not the example of Jesus, but the redeeming work of Jesus, was the primary thing for Paul. The religion of Paul was not primarily faith in God like Jesus' faith; it was faith in Jesus; Paul committed to Jesus without reserve the eternal destinies of his soul. That is what we mean when we say that Paul stood in a truly religious relation to Jesus.

But Paul was not the first to stand in this religious relation to Jesus. Evidently, at this decisive point, he was only continuing an attitude toward Jesus which had already been assumed by those who had been Christians before him. Paul was not indeed led to assume that attitude by the persuasions of the earlier disciples; he was converted by the Lord Himself on the road to Damascus. But the faith so induced was in essentials like the faith which had already prevailed among the earlier disciples. Indeed, an account of the redeeming work of Christ is designated by Paul as something that he had "received"; and that account had evidently been accompanied already in the primitive Church by trust in the Redeemer. Paul was not the first who had faith in Jesus, as distinguished from faith in God like the faith which Jesus had; Paul was not the first to make Jesus the object of faith.

So much will no doubt be admitted by all. But who were the predecessors of Paul in making Jesus the object of faith? The obvious answer has always been that they were the primitive disciples in Jerusalem, and that answer really stands abundantly firm. A strange attempt has indeed been made in recent years, by Bousset and Heitmüller, to cast doubt upon it. What Paul "received," it has been suggested, was received, not from the primitive Jerusalem Church, but from such Christian communities as the one at Antioch. But this attempt at interposing an extra link between the Jerusalem Church and Paul has resulted in failure. The Epistles really provide abundant information as to Paul's relations to Jerusalem. Paul was deeply interested in the Jerusalem Church; in opposition to his Judaizing opponents, who had in certain matters appealed to the original apostles against him, he emphasizes his agreement with Peter and the rest. But even the Judaizers had had no objection to Paul's way of regarding Jesus as the object of faith; about that matter there is not in the Epistles the least suspicion of any debate. About the place of the Mosaic law in the Christian life there was discussion, though even with regard to that matter the Judaizers were entirely unjustified in appealing to the original apostles against Paul. But with regard to the attitude toward Jesus the original apostles had evidently given not even the slightest color for an appeal to them against the teaching of Paul. Evidently in making Jesus the object of religious faith—the thing that was the heart and soul of Paul's religion—Paul was in no disagreement with those who had been apostles before him. Had there been such disagreement, the "right hand of fellowship," which the pillars of the Jerusalem Church gave to Paul (Gal. ii. 9), would have been impossible. The facts are really too plain. The whole of early Christian history is a hopeless riddle unless the Jerusalem Church, as well as Paul, made Jesus the object of religious faith. Primitive Christianity certainly did not consist in the mere imitation of Jesus.

But was this "faith in Jesus" justified by the teaching of Jesus Himself? The question has really been answered in Chapter II. It was there shown that Jesus most certainly did not keep His Person out of His gospel, but on the contrary presented Himself as the Saviour of men. The demonstration of that fact was the highest merit of the late James Denney. His work on "Jesus and the Gospel" is faulty in some respects; it is marred by an undue concessiveness toward some modern types of criticism. But just because of its concessiveness with regard to many important matters, its main thesis stands all the more firm. Denney has shown that no matter what view be taken of the sources underlying the Gospels, and no matter what elements in the Gospels be rejected as secondary, still even the supposed "historical Jesus," as He is left after the critical process is done, plainly presented Himself, not merely as an example for faith, but as the object of faith.

It may be added, moreover, that Jesus did not invite the confidence of men by minimizing the load which He offered to bear. He did not say: "Trust me to give you acceptance with God, because acceptance with God is not difficult; God does not regard sin so seriously after all." On the contrary Jesus presented the wrath of God in a more awful way than it was afterwards presented by His disciples; it was Jesus—Jesus whom modern liberals represent as a mild-mannered exponent of an indiscriminating love—it was Jesus who spoke of the outer darkness and the everlasting fire, of the sin that shall not be forgiven either in this world or in that which is to come. There is nothing in Jesus' teaching about the character of God which in itself can evoke trust. On the contrary the awful presentation can give rise, in the hearts of us sinners, only to despair. Trust arises only when we attend to God's way of salvation. And that way is found in Jesus. Jesus did not invite the confidence of men by a minimizing presentation of what was necessary in order that sinners might stand faultless before the awful throne of God. On the contrary, he invited confidence by the presentation of His own wondrous Person. Great was the guilt of sin, but Jesus was greater still. God, according to Jesus, was a loving Father; but He was a loving Father, not of the sinful world, but of those whom He Himself had brought into His Kingdom through the Son.

The truth is, the witness of the New Testament, with regard to Jesus as the object of faith, is an absolutely unitary witness. The thing is rooted far too deep in the records of primitive Christianity ever to be removed by any critical process. The Jesus spoken of in the New Testament was no mere teacher of righteousness, no mere pioneer in a new type of religious life, but One who was regarded, and regarded Himself, as the Saviour whom men could trust.

But by modern liberalism He is regarded in a totally different way. Christians stand in a religious relation to Jesus; liberals do not stand in a religious relation to Jesus—what difference could be more profound than that? The modern liberal preacher reverences Jesus; he has the name of Jesus forever on his lips; he speaks of Jesus as the supreme revelation of God; he enters, or tries to enter, into the religious life of Jesus. But he does not stand in a religious relation to Jesus. Jesus for him is an example for faith, not the object of faith. The modern liberal tries to have faith in God like the faith which he supposes Jesus had in God; but he does not have faith in Jesus.

According to modern liberalism, in other words, Jesus was the Founder of Christianity because He was the first Christian, and Christianity consists in maintenance of the religious life which Jesus instituted.

But was Jesus really a Christian? Or, to put the same question in another way, are we able or ought we as Christians to enter in every respect into the experience of Jesus and make Him in every respect our example? Certain difficulties arise with regard to this question.

The first difficulty appears in the Messianic consciousness of Jesus. The Person whom we are asked to take as our example thought that He was the heavenly Son of

Man who was to be the final Judge of all the earth. **Can**
we imitate Him there? The trouble is not merely that
Jesus undertook a special mission which can never be ours.
That difficulty might conceivably be overcome; we might
still take Jesus as our example by adapting to our station
in life the kind of character which He displayed in His.
But another difficulty is more serious. The real trouble is
that the lofty claim of Jesus, if, as modern liberalism is
constrained to believe, the claim was unjustified, places a
moral stain upon Jesus' character. What shall be thought
of a human being who lapsed so far from the path of
humility and sanity as to believe that the eternal destinies
of the world were committed into His hands? The truth
is that if Jesus be merely an example, He is not a worthy
example; for He claimed to be far more.

Against this objection modern liberalism has usually
adopted a policy of palliation. The Messianic consciousness, it is said, arose late in the experience of Jesus, and
was not really fundamental. What was really fundamental, the liberal historians continue, was the consciousness
of sonship toward God—a consciousness which may be
shared by every humble disciple. The Messianic consciousness, on this view, arose only as an afterthought.
Jesus was conscious, it is said, of standing toward God in
a relation of untroubled sonship. But He discovered that
this relation was not shared by others. He became aware,
therefore, of a mission to bring others into the place of
privilege which He Himself already occupied. That mission made Him unique, and to give expression to His
uniqueness He adopted, late in His life and almost against
His will, the faulty category of Messiahship.

Many are the forms in which some such psychological
reconstruction of the life of Jesus has been set forth in
recent years. The modern world has devoted its very best

literary efforts to this task. But the efforts have resulted
in failure. In the first place, there is no real evidence that
the reconstructed Jesus is historical. The sources know
nothing of a Jesus who adopted the category of Messiahship late in life and against His will. On the contrary the
only Jesus that they present is a Jesus who based the
whole of His ministry upon His stupendous claim. In the
second place, even if the modern reconstruction were historical it would not solve the problem at all. The problem
is a moral and psychological problem. How can a human
being who lapsed so far from the path of rectitude as to
think Himself to be the judge of all the earth—how can
such a human being be regarded as the supreme example
for mankind? It is absolutely no answer to the objection
to say that Jesus accepted the category of Messiahship
reluctantly and late in life. No matter when He suc-
cumbed to temptation the outstanding fact is that, on this
view, He did succumb; and that moral defeat places an
indelible stain upon His character. No doubt it is possible to make excuses for Him, and many excuses are as a
matter of fact made by the liberal historians. But what
has become then of the claim of liberalism to be truly
Christian? Can a man for whom excuses have to be made
be regarded as standing to his modern critics in a relationship even remotely analogous to that in which the Jesus
of the New Testament stands to the Christian Church?

But there is another difficulty in the way of regarding
Jesus as simply the first Christian. This second difficulty
concerns the attitude of Jesus toward sin. If Jesus is
separated from us by his Messianic consciousness, He is
separated from us even more fundamentally by the
absence in Him of a sense of sin.

With respect to the sinlessness of Jesus modern liberal
historians find themselves in a quandary. To affirm that

He was sinless means to relinquish much of that ease of defending liberal religion which the liberal historians are anxious to preserve, and involves hazardous assumptions with regard to the nature of sin. For if sin is merely imperfection, how can an absolute negation of it be ventured upon within a process of nature which is supposed to be ever changing and ever advancing? The very idea of "sinlessness," much more the reality of it, requires us to conceive of sin as transgression of a fixed law or a fixed standard, and involves the conception of an absolute goodness. But to that conception of an *absolute* goodness the modern evolutionary view of the world properly speaking has no right. At any rate, if such absolute goodness is to be allowed to intrude at a definite point in the present world-process, we are involved in that supernaturalism which, as will be observed later, is the very thing that the modern reconstruction of Christianity is most anxious to avoid. Once affirm that Jesus was sinless and all other men sinful, and you have entered into irreconcilable conflict with the whole modern point of view. On the other hand, if there are scientific objections, from the liberal point of view, against an affirmation of the sinlessness of Jesus, there are also very obvious religious objections against an opposite affirmation of His sinfulness—difficulties for modern liberalism as well as for the theology of the historic Church. If Jesus was sinful like other men, the last remnant of his uniqueness would seem to have disappeared, and all continuity with the previous development of Christianity would seem to be destroyed.

In the face of this quandary the modern liberal historian is inclined to avoid rash assertions. He will not be sure that when Jesus taught His disciples to say, "Forgive us our debts," He did not pray that prayer with them; on the other hand he will not really face the results that logically follow from his doubt. In his perplexity, he is apt to be content with the assertion that whether Jesus was sinless or not He was at any rate immeasurably above the rest of us. Whether Jesus was "sinless" is an academic question, we shall probably be told, that concerns the mysteries of the absolute; what we need to do is to bow in simple reverence before a holiness which compared with our impurity is as a white light in a dark place.

That such avoidance of the difficulty is unsatisfactory hardly requires proof; obviously the liberal theologian is trying to obtain the religious advantages of an affirmation of sinlessness in Jesus at the same time that he obtains the supposed scientific advantages of its denial. But just for the moment we are not concerned with the question at all; we are not concerned to determine whether as a matter of fact Jesus was sinless or no. What we need to observe just now is that whether Jesus was sinful or sinless at any rate in the record of His life which has actually come into our hands He displays no consciousness of sin. Even if the words "Why callest thou me good?" meant that Jesus denied the attribute of goodness to Himself—which they do not—it would still remain true that He never in His recorded words deals in any intelligible way with sin in His own life. In the account of the temptation we are told how He kept sin from entering, but never how He dealt with it after its entrance had been effected. The religious experience of Jesus, as it is recorded in the Gospels, in other words, gives us no information about the way in which sin shall be removed.

Yet in the Gospels Jesus is represented constantly as dealing with the problem of sin. He always assumes that other men are sinful; yet He never finds sin in Himself. A stupendous difference is found here between Jesus' experience and ours.

That difference prevents the religious experience of Jesus from serving as the sole basis of the Christian life. For clearly if Christianity is anything it is a way of getting rid of sin. At any rate, if it is not that it is useless; for all men have sinned. And as a matter of fact it *was* that from the very beginning. Whether the beginning of Christian preaching be put on the day of Pentecost or when Jesus first taught in Galilee, in either case one of its first words was "Repent." Throughout the whole New Testament the Christianity of the primitive Church is represented clearly as a way of getting rid of sin. But if Christianity is a way of getting rid of sin, then Jesus was not a Christian; for Jesus, so far as we can see, had no sin to get rid of.

Why then did the early Christians call themselves disciples of Jesus, why did they connect themselves with His name? The answer is not difficult. They connected themselves with His name not because He was their example in their ridding themselves of sin, but because their method of ridding themselves of sin was by means of Him. It was what Jesus did for them, and not primarily the example of His own life, which made them Christians. Such is the witness of all our primitive records. The record is fullest, as has already been observed, in the case of the Apostle Paul; clearly Paul regarded himself as saved from sin by what Jesus did for him on the cross. But Paul did not stand alone. "Christ died *for our sins*" was not something that Paul had originated; it was something he had "received." The benefits of that saving work of Christ, according to the primitive Church, were to be received by faith; even if the classic formulation of this conviction should prove to be due to Paul, the conviction itself clearly goes back to the very beginning. The primitive Christians felt themselves in need of salvation. How, they asked, should the load of sin be removed? Their answer is perfectly plain. They simply trusted Jesus to remove it. In other words they had "faith" in Him.

Here again we are brought face to face with the significant fact which was noticed at the beginning of this chapter; the early Christians regarded Jesus not merely as an example for faith but primarily as the object of faith. Christianity from the beginning was a means of getting rid of sin by trust in Jesus of Nazareth. But if Jesus was thus the object of Christian faith, He Himself was no more a Christian than God is a religious being. God is the object of all religion, He is absolutely necessary to all religion; but He Himself is the only being in the universe who can never in His own nature be religious. So it is with Jesus as related to Christian faith. Christian faith is trust reposed in Him for the removal of sin; He could not repose trust (in the sense with which we are here concerned) in Himself; therefore He was certainly not a Christian. If we are looking for a complete illustration of the Christian life we cannot find it in the religious experience of Jesus.

This conclusion needs to be guarded against two objections.

In the first place, it will be said, are we not failing to do justice to the true humanity of Jesus, which is affirmed by the creeds of the Church as well as by the modern theologians? When we say that Jesus could not illustrate Christian faith any more than God can be religious, are we not denying to Jesus that religious experience which is a necessary element in true humanity? Must not Jesus, if He be true man, have been more than the object of religious faith; must He not have had a religion of His own? The answer is not far to seek. Certainly Jesus had a religion of His own; His prayer was real prayer, His

faith was real religious faith. His relation to His heavenly Father was not merely that of a child to a father;
it was that of a man to his God. Certainly Jesus had a
religion; without it His humanity would indeed have been
but incomplete. Without doubt Jesus had a religion; the
fact is of the utmost importance. But it is equally important to observe that that religion which Jesus had
was not Christianity. Christianity is a way of getting
rid of sin, and Jesus was without sin. His religion was a
religion of Paradise, not a religion of sinful humanity.
It was a religion to which we may perhaps in some sort
attain in heaven, when the process of our purification is
complete (though even then the memory of redemption
will never leave us); but certainly it is not a religion with
which we can begin. The religion of Jesus was a religion
of untroubled sonship; Christianity is a religion of the
attainment of sonship by the redeeming work of Christ.

But if that be true, it may be objected, in the second
place, that Jesus is being removed far from us, that on
our view He is no longer our Brother and our Example.
The objection is welcome, since it helps us to avoid misunderstandings and exaggerations.

Certainly if our zeal for the greatness and uniqueness
of Jesus led us so to separate Him from us that He could
no longer be touched with the feeling of our infirmities, the
result would be disastrous; Jesus' coming would lose
much of its significance. But it ought to be observed that
likeness is not always necessary to nearness. The experience of a father in his personal relation to his son is quite
different from that of the son in his relation to his father;
but just that very difference binds father and son all the
more closely together. The father cannot share the specifically filial affection of the son, and the son cannot
share the specifically paternal affection of the father:

yet no mere relationship of brotherhood, perhaps, could be quite so close. Fatherhood and sonship are complementary to each other; hence the dissimilarity, but hence also the closeness of the bond. It may be somewhat the same in the case of our relationship to Jesus. If He were exactly the same as ourselves, if He were merely our Brother, we should not be nearly so close to Him as we are when He stands to us in the relationship of a Saviour.

Nevertheless Jesus as a matter of fact is a Brother to us as well as a Saviour—an elder Brother whose steps we may follow. The imitation of Jesus has a fundamental place in Christian life; it is perfectly correct to represent Him as our supreme and only perfect example.

Certainly so far as the field of ethics is concerned, there can be no dispute. No matter what view may be taken of His origin and His higher nature, Jesus certainly led a true human life, and in it He came into those varied human relationships which provide opportunity for moral achievement. His life of perfect purity was led in no cold aloofness from the throng and press; His unselfish love was exercised not merely in mighty deeds, but in acts of kindness which the humblest of us has the power, if only we had the will, to imitate. More effective, too, than all detail is the indefinable impression of the whole; Jesus is felt to be far greater than any of His individual words or deeds. His calmness, unselfishness and strength have been the wonder of the ages; the world can never lose the inspiration of that radiant example.

Jesus is an example, moreover, not merely for the relations of man to man but also for the relation of man to God; imitation of Him may extend and must extend to the sphere of religion as well as to that of ethics. Indeed religion and ethics in Him were never separated; no single element in His life can be understood without reference to His heavenly Father. Jesus was the most religious man who ever lived; He did nothing and said nothing and thought nothing without the thought of God. If His example means anything at all it means that a human life without the conscious presence of God—even though it be a life of humanitarian service outwardly like the ministry of Jesus—is a monstrous perversion. If we would follow truly in Jesus' steps, we must obey the first commandment as well as the second that is like unto it; we must love the Lord our God with all our heart and soul and mind and strength. The difference between Jesus and ourselves serves only to enforce, certainly not to invalidate, the lesson. If the One to whom all power was given needed refreshment and strengthening in prayer, we more; if the One to whom the lilies of the field revealed the glory of God yet went into the sanctuary, surely we need such assistance even more than He; if the wise and holy One could say "Thy will be done," surely submission is yet more in place for us whose wisdom is as the foolishness of children.

Thus Jesus is the supreme example for men. But the Jesus who can serve as an example is not the Jesus of modern liberal reconstruction, but only the Jesus of the New Testament. The Jesus of modern liberalism advanced stupendous claims which were not founded upon fact—such conduct ought never to be made a norm. The Jesus of modern liberalism all through His ministry employed language which was extravagant and absurd— and it is only to be hoped that imitation of Him will not lead to an equal extravagance in His modern disciples. If the Jesus of naturalistic reconstruction were really taken as an example, disaster would soon follow. As a matter of fact, however, the modern liberal does not really take as his example the Jesus of the liberal historians;

what he really does in practice is to manufacture as his example a simple exponent of a non-doctrinal religion whom the abler historians even of his own school know never to have existed except in the imagination of modern men. Very different is the imitation of the real Jesus—the Jesus of the New Testament who actually lived in the first century of our era. That Jesus advanced lofty claims; but His claims, instead of being the extravagant dreams of an enthusiast, were sober truth. On His lips, therefore, language which in the reduced Jesus of modern reconstruction would be frenzied or absurd becomes fraught with blessing for mankind. Jesus demanded that those who followed Him should be willing to break even the holiest ties—He said, "If a man cometh to me and hateth not his father and mother . . . he cannot be my disciple," and "Let the dead bury their dead." Coming from the mere prophet constructed by modern liberalism, those words would be monstrous; coming from the real Jesus, they are sublime. How great was the mission of mercy which justified such words! And how wonderful the condescension of the eternal Son! How matchless an example for the children of men! Well might Paul appeal to the example of the incarnate Saviour; well might he say, "Let the same mind be in you which was also in Christ Jesus." The imitation of the real Jesus will never lead a man astray.

But the example of Jesus is a perfect example only if He was justified in what He offered to men. And He offered, not primarily guidance, but salvation; He presented Himself as the object of men's faith. That offer is rejected by modern liberalism, but it is accepted by Christian men.

There is a profound difference, then, in the attitude

assumed by modern liberalism and by Christianity toward Jesus the Lord. Liberalism regards Him as an Example and Guide; Christianity, as a Saviour: liberalism makes Him an example for faith; Christianity, the object of faith.

This difference in the attitude toward Jesus depends upon a profound difference as to the question who Jesus was. If Jesus was only what the liberal historians suppose that He was, then trust in Him would be out of place; our attitude toward Him could be that of pupils to a Master and nothing more. But if He was what the New Testament represents Him as being, then we can safely commit to Him the eternal destinies of our souls. What then is the difference between liberalism and Christianity with regard to the person of our Lord?

The answer might be difficult to set forth in detail. But the essential thing can be put almost in a word—liberalism regards Jesus as the fairest flower of humanity; Christianity regards Him as a supernatural Person.

The conception of Jesus as a supernatural Person runs all through the New Testament. In the Epistles of Paul, of course, it is quite clear. Without the slightest doubt Paul separated Jesus from ordinary humanity and placed Him on the side of God. The words in Gal. i. 1, "not from men nor through a man but through Jesus Christ and God the Father who raised Him from the dead," are only typical of what appears everywhere in the Epistles. The same contrast between Jesus Christ and ordinary humanity is everywhere presupposed. Paul does indeed call Jesus Christ a man. But the way in which he speaks of Jesus as a man only deepens the impression which has already been received. Paul speaks of the humanity of Jesus apparently as though the fact that Jesus was a man were something strange, something wonderful. At

any rate, the really outstanding fact is that in the
Epistles of Paul, Jesus is everywhere separated from
ordinary humanity; the deity of Christ is everywhere presupposed. It is a matter of small consequence whether
Paul ever applies to Jesus the Greek word which is trans-
lated "God" in the English Bible; certainly it is very
difficult, in view of Rom. ix. 5, to deny that he does.
However that may be, the term "Lord," which is Paul's
regular designation of Jesus, is really just as much a
designation of deity as is the term "God." It was a designation of deity even in the pagan religions with which
Paul's converts were familiar; and (what is far more important) in the Greek translation of the Old Testament
which was current in Paul's day and was used by the
Apostle himself, the term was used to translate the
"Jahwe" of the Hebrew text. And Paul does not hesitate
to apply to Jesus stupendous passages in the Greek Old
Testament where the term Lord thus designates the God
of Israel. But what is perhaps most significant of all for
the establishment of the Pauline teaching about the Person of Christ is that Paul everywhere stands in a religious
attitude toward Jesus. He who is thus the object of
religious faith is surely no mere man, but a supernatural
Person, and indeed a Person who was God.

Thus Paul regarded Jesus as a supernatural Person.
The fact would be surprising if it stood alone. Paul was
a contemporary of Jesus. What must this Jesus have
been that He should be lifted thus quickly above the limits
of ordinary humanity and placed upon the side of God?

But there is something far more surprising still. The
truly surprising thing is that the view which Paul had of
Jesus was also the view which was held by Jesus' intimate
friends.[1] The fact appears in the Pauline Epistles them-

[1] Compare *The Origin of Paul's Religion*, 1921, pp. 118-137.

selves, to say nothing of other evidence. Clearly the Epistles presuppose a fundamental unity between Paul and the original apostles with regard to the Person of Christ; for if there had been any controversy about this matter it would certainly have been mentioned. Even the Judaizers, the bitter opponents of Paul, seem to have had no objection to Paul's conception of Jesus as a supernatural Person. The really impressive thing about Paul's view of Christ is that it is not defended. Indeed it is hardly presented in the Epistles in any systematic way. Yet it is everywhere presupposed. The inference is perfectly plain—Paul's conception of the Person of Christ was a matter of course in the primitive Church. With regard to this matter Paul appears in perfect harmony with all Palestinian Christians. The men who had walked and talked with Jesus and had seen Him subject to the petty limitations of earthly life agreed with Paul fully in regarding Him as a supernatural Person, seated on the throne of all Being.

Exactly the same account of Jesus as that which is presupposed by the Pauline Epistles appears in the detailed narrative of the Gospels. The Gospels agree with Paul in presenting Jesus as a supernatural Person, and the agreement appears not in one or two of the Gospels, but in all four. The day is long past, if there ever was such a day, when the Gospel of John, as presenting a divine Jesus, could be contrasted with the Gospel of Mark, as presenting a human Jesus. On the contrary, all four Gospels clearly present a Person lifted far above the level of ordinary humanity; and the Gospel of Mark, the shortest and according to modern criticism the earliest of the Gospels, renders particularly prominent Jesus' superhuman works of power. In all four Gospels Jesus appears possessed of a sovereign power over the forces of nature; in all four Gospels, as in the whole New Testament, He appears clearly as a supernatural Person.[1]

But what is meant by a "supernatural Person"; what is meant by the supernatural?

The conception of the "supernatural" is closely connected with that of "miracle"; a miracle is the supernatural manifesting itself in the external world. But what is the supernatural? Many definitions have been proposed. But only one definition is really correct. A supernatural event is one that takes place by the immediate, as distinguished from the mediate, power of God. The possibility of the supernatural, if supernatural be defined in this way, presupposes two things—it presupposes (1) the existence of a personal God, and (2) the existence of a real order of nature. Without the existence of a personal God, there could be no purposive entrance of God's power into the order of the world; and without the real existence of an order of nature there could be no distinction between natural events and those that are above nature— all events would be supernatural, or rather the word "supernatural" would have no meaning at all. The distinction between "natural" and "supernatural" does not mean, indeed, that nature is independent of God; it does not mean that while God brings to pass supernatural events, natural events are not brought to pass by Him. On the contrary, the believer in the supernatural regards everything that is done as being the work of God. Only, he believes that in the events called natural, God uses means, whereas in the events called supernatural He uses no means, but puts forth His creative power. The distinction between the natural and the supernatural, in other words, is simply the distinction between God's works of providence and God's work of creation; a miracle is a

[1] Compare *History and Faith*, 1915, pp. 5f.

work of creation just as truly as the mysterious act which produced the world.

This conception of the supernatural depends absolutely upon a theistic view of God. Theism is to be distinguished (1) from deism and (2) from pantheism.

According to the deistic view, God set the world going like a machine and then left it independent of Himself. Such a view is inconsistent with the actuality of the supernatural; the miracles of the Bible presuppose a God who is constantly watching over and guiding the course of this world. The miracles of the Bible are not arbitrary intrusions of a Power that is without relation to the world, but are evidently intended to accomplish results within the order of nature. Indeed the natural and the supernatural are blended, in the miracles of the Bible, in a way entirely incongruous with the deistic conception of God. In the feeding of the five thousand, for example, who shall say what part the five loaves and two fishes had in the event; who shall say where the natural left off and the supernatural began? Yet that event, if any, surely transcended the order of nature. The miracles of the Bible, then, are not the work of a God who has no part in the course of nature; they are the work of a God who through His works of providence is "preserving and governing all His creatures and all their actions."

But the conception of the supernatural is inconsistent, not only with deism, but also with pantheism. Pantheism identifies God with the totality of nature. It is inconceivable, then, on the pantheistic view that anything should enter into the course of nature from outside. A similar incongruity with the supernatural appears also in certain forms of idealism, which deny real existence to the forces of nature. If what seems to be connected in nature is really only connected in the divine mind, then it

is difficult to make any distinction between those opera·
tions of the divine mind which appear as miracles and
those which appear as natural events. Again, it has often
been said that all events are works of creation. On this
view, it is only a concession to popular phraseology to say
that one body is attracted toward another in accordance
with a law of gravitation; what really ought to be said is
that when two bodies are in proximity under certain conditions they come together. Certain phenomena in nature,
on this view, are always followed by certain other phenomena, and it is really only this regularity of sequence
which is indicated by the assertion that the former phenomena "cause" the latter; the only real cause is in all
cases God. On the basis of this view, there can be no
distinction between events wrought by the immediate
power of God and those that are not; for on this view all
events are so wrought. Against such a view, those who
accept our definition of miracle will naturally accept the
common-sense notion of cause. God is always the first
cause, but there are truly second causes; and they are the
means which God uses, in the ordinary course of the world,
for the accomplishment of His ends. It is the exclusion of
such second causes which makes an event a miracle.

It is sometimes said that the actuality of miracles
would destroy the basis of science. Science, it is said, is
founded upon the regularity of sequences; it assumes that
if certain conditions within the course of nature are given,
certain other conditions will always follow. But if there
is to be any intrusion of events which by their very definition are independent of all previous conditions, then, it is
said, the regularity of nature upon which science bases
itself is broken up. Miracle, in other words, seems to
introduce an element of arbitrariness and unaccountabil-
ity into the course of the world.

The objection ignores what is really fundamental in the Christian conception of miracle. According to the Christian conception, a miracle is wrought by the immediate power of God. It is not wrought by an arbitrary and fantastic despot, but by the very God to whom the regularity of nature itself is due—by the God, moreover, whose character is known through the Bible. Such a God, we may be sure, will not do despite to the reason that He has given to His creatures; His interposition will introduce no disorder into the world that He has made. There is nothing arbitrary about a miracle, according to the Christian conception. It is not an uncaused event, but an event that is caused by the very source of all the order that is in the world. It is dependent altogether upon the least arbitrary and the most firmly fixed of all the things that are—namely upon the character of God.

The possibility of miracle, then, is indissolubly joined with "theism." Once admit the existence of a personal God, Maker and Ruler of the world, and no limits, temporal or otherwise, can be set to the creative power of such a God. Admit that God once created the world, and you cannot deny that He might engage in creation again. But it will be said, the actuality of miracles is different from the possibility of them. It may be admitted that miracles conceivably might occur. But have they actually occurred?

This question looms very large in the minds of modern men. The burden of the question seems to rest heavily even upon many who still accept the miracles of the New Testament. The miracles used to be regarded as an aid to faith, it is often said, but now they are a hindrance to faith; faith used to come on account of the miracles, but now it comes in despite of them; men used to believe in

Jesus because He wrought miracles, but now we accept
the miracles because on other grounds we have come to
believe in Him.

A strange confusion underlies this common way of
speaking. In one sense, certainly, miracles are a hindrance to faith—but who ever thought the contrary? It
may certainly be admitted that if the New Testament
narrative had no miracles in it, it would be far easier to
believe. The more commonplace a story is, the easier it is
to accept it as true. But commonplace narratives have
little value. The New Testament without the miracles
would be far easier to believe. But the trouble is, it
would not be worth believing. Without the miracles the
New Testament would contain an account of a holy man
—not a perfect man, it is true, for He was led to make
lofty claims to which He had no right—but a man at least
far holier than the rest of men. But of what benefit would
such a man, and the death which marked His failure, be to
us? The loftier be the example which Jesus set, the
greater becomes our sorrow at our failure to attain to it;
and the greater our hopelessness under the burden of sin.
The sage of Nazareth may satisfy those who have never
faced the problem of evil in their own lives; but to talk
about an ideal to those who are under the thralldom of
sin is a cruel mockery. Yet if Jesus was merely a man
like the rest of men, then an ideal is all that we have in
Him. Far more is needed by a sinful world. It is small
comfort to be told that there was goodness in the world,
when what we need is goodness triumphant over sin. But
goodness triumphant over sin involves an entrance of the
creative power of God, and that creative power of God is
manifested by the miracles. Without the miracles, the
New Testament might be easier to believe. But the thing
that would be believed would be entirely different from

that which presents itself to us now. Without the miracles we should have a teacher; with the miracles we have a Saviour.

Certainly it is a mistake to isolate the miracles from the rest of the New Testament. It is a mistake to discuss the question of the resurrection of Jesus as though that which is to be proved were simply the resurrection of a certain man of the first century in Palestine. No doubt the existing evidence for such an event, strong as the evidence is, might be insufficient. The historian would indeed be obliged to say that no naturalistic explanation of the origin of the Church has yet been discovered, and that the evidence for the miracle is exceedingly strong; but miracles are, to say the least, extremely unusual events, and there is a tremendous hostile presumption against accepting the hypothesis of miracle in any given case. But as a matter of fact, the question in this case does not concern the resurrection of a man about whom we know nothing; it concerns the resurrection of Jesus. And Jesus was certainly a very extraordinary Person. The uniqueness of the character of Jesus removes the hostile presumption against miracle; it was extremely improbable that any ordinary man should rise from the dead, but Jesus was like no other man that ever lived.

But the evidence for the miracles of the New Testament is supported in yet another way; it is supported by the existence of an adequate occasion. It has been observed above that a miracle is an event produced by the immediate power of God, and that God is a God of order. The evidence of a miracle is therefore enormously strengthened when the purpose of the miracle can be detected. That does not mean that within a complex of miracles an exact reason must be assigned to every one; it does not mean that in the New Testament we should expect to see exactly why a miracle was wrought in one case and not in another. But it does mean that acceptance of a complex of miracles is made vastly easier when an adequate reason can be detected for the complex as a whole. In the case of the New Testament miracles, such an adequate reason is not difficult to find. It is found in the conquest of sin. According to the Christian view, as set forth in the Bible, mankind is under the curse of God's holy law, and the dreadful penalty includes the corruption of our whole nature. Actual transgressions proceed from the sinful root, and serve to deepen every man's guilt in the sight of God. On the basis of that view, so profound, so true to the observed facts of life, it is obvious that nothing natural will meet our need. Nature transmits the dreadful taint; hope is to be sought only in a creative act of God.

And that creative act of God—so mysterious, so contrary to all expectation, yet so congruous with the character of the God who is revealed as the God of love—is found in the redeeming work of Christ. No product of sinful humanity could have redeemed humanity from the dreadful guilt or lifted a sinful race from the slough of sin. But a Saviour has come from God. There lies the very root of the Christian religion; there is the reason why the supernatural is the very ground and substance of the Christian faith.

But the acceptance of the supernatural depends upon a conviction of the reality of sin. Without the conviction of sin there can be no appreciation of the uniqueness of Jesus; it is only when we contrast our sinfulness with His holiness that we appreciate the gulf which separates Him from the rest of the children of men. And without the conviction of sin there can be no understanding of the occasion for the supernatural act of God; without the

conviction of sin, the good news of redemption seems to
be an idle tale. So fundamental is the conviction of sin
in the Christian faith that it will not do to arrive at it
merely by a process of reasoning; it will not do to say
merely: All men (as I have been told) are sinners; I am
a man; therefore I suppose I must be a sinner too. That
is all the supposed conviction of sin amounts to sometimes. But the true conviction is far more immediate
than that. It depends indeed upon information that comes
from without; it depends upon the revelation of the law
of God; it depends upon the awful verities set forth in
the Bible as to the universal sinfulness of mankind. But
it adds to the revelation that has come from without a
conviction of the whole mind and heart, a profound understanding of one's own lost condition, an illumination of
the deadened conscience which causes a Copernican revolution in one's attitude toward the world and toward
God. When a man has passed through that experience,
he wonders at his former blindness. And especially does
he wonder at his former attitude toward the miracles of
the New Testament, and toward the supernatural Person
who is there revealed. The truly penitent man glories in
the supernatural, for he knows that nothing natural would
meet his need; the world has been shaken once in his
downfall, and shaken again it must be if he is to be saved.

Yet an acceptance of the presuppositions of miracle
does not render unnecessary the plain testimony to the
miracles that have actually occurred. And that testimony is exceedingly strong.[1] The Jesus presented in the
New Testament was clearly an historical Person—so
much is admitted by all who have really come to grips
with the historical problems at all. But just as clearly
the Jesus presented in the New Testament was a super-

[1] Compare *History and Faith*, 1915, pp. 6-8.

natural Person. Yet for modern liberalism a supernatural person is never historical. A problem arises then for those who adopt the liberal point of view—the Jesus of the New Testament is historical, He is supernatural, and yet what is supernatural, on the liberal hypothesis, can never be historical. The problem could be solved only by the separation of the natural from the supernatural in the New Testament account of Jesus, in order that what is supernatural might be rejected and what is natural might be retained. But the process of separation has never been successfully carried out. Many have been the attempts—the modern liberal Church has put its very heart and soul into the effort, so that there is scarcely any more brilliant chapter in the history of the human spirit than this "quest of the historical Jesus"—but all the attempts have failed. The trouble is that the miracles are found not to be an excrescence in the New Testament account of Jesus, but belong to the very warp and woof. They are intimately connected with Jesus' lofty claims; they stand or fall with the undoubted purity of His character; they reveal the very nature of His mission in the world.

Yet miracles are rejected by the modern liberal Church, and with the miracles the entirety of the supernatural Person of our Lord. Not some miracles are rejected, but all. It is a matter of no importance whatever that some of the wonderful works of Jesus are accepted by the liberal Church; it means absolutely nothing when some of the works of healing are regarded as historical. For those works are no longer regarded by modern liberalism as supernatural, but merely as faith-cures of an extraordinary kind. And it is the presence or absence of the true supernatural which is the really important thing. Such concessions as to faith-cures, moreover, carry us at best but a very short way—disbelievers in the supernatural must simply reject as legendary or mythical the great mass of the wonderful works.

The question, then, does not concern the historicity of this miracle or that; it concerns the historicity of all miracles. That fact is often obscured, and the obscuration of it often introduces an element of something like disingenuousness into the advocacy of the liberal cause. The liberal preacher singles out some one miracle and discusses that as though it were the only point at issue. The miracle which is usually singled out is the Virgin Birth. The liberal preacher insists on the possibility of believing in Christ no matter which view be adopted as to the manner of His entrance into the world. Is not the Person the same no matter how He was born? The impression is thus produced upon the plain man that the preacher is accepting the main outlines of the New Testament account of Jesus, but merely has difficulties with this particular element in the account. But such an impression is radically false. It is true that some men have denied the Virgin Birth and yet have accepted the New Testament account of Jesus as a supernatural Person. But such men are exceedingly few and far between. It might be difficult to find a single one of any prominence living to-day, so profoundly and so obviously congruous is the Virgin Birth with the whole New Testament presentation of Christ. The overwhelming majority of those who reject the Virgin Birth reject also the whole supernatural content of the New Testament, and make of the "resurrection" just what the word "resurrection" most emphatically did not mean—a permanence of the influence of Jesus or a mere spiritual existence of Jesus beyond the grave. Old words may here be used, but the thing that they designate is gone. The disciples believed in the con-

tinued personal existence of Jesus even during the three
sad days after the crucifixion; they were not Sadducees;
they believed that Jesus lived and would rise at the last
day. But what enabled them to begin the work of the
Christian Church was that they believed the body of Jesus
already to have been raised from the tomb by the power
of God. That belief involves the acceptance of the supernatural; and the acceptance of the supernatural is thus
the very heart and soul of the religion that we profess.

Whatever decision is made, the issue should certainly
not be obscured. The issue does not concern individual
miracles, even so important a miracle as the Virgin Birth.
It really concerns all miracles. And the question concerning all miracles is simply the question of the acceptance or
rejection of the Saviour that the New Testament presents.
Reject the miracles and you have in Jesus the fairest
flower of humanity who made such an impression upon
His followers that after His death they could not believe
that He had perished but experienced hallucinations in
which they thought they saw Him risen from the dead;
accept the miracles, and you have a Saviour who came
voluntarily into this world for our salvation, suffered for
our sins upon the Cross, rose again from the dead by the
power of God, and ever lives to make intercession for us.
The difference between those two views is the difference
between two totally diverse religions. It is high time that
this issue should be faced; it is high time that the misleading use of traditional phrases should be abandoned and
men should speak their full mind. Shall we accept the
Jesus of the New Testament as our Saviour, or shall we
reject Him with the liberal Church?

At this point an objection may be raised. The liberal
preacher, it may be said, is often ready to speak of the
"deity" of Christ; he is often ready to say that "Jesus

is God." The plain man is much impressed. The preacher, he says, believes in the deity of our Lord; obviously then his unorthodoxy must concern only details; and those who object to his presence in the Church are narrow and uncharitable heresy-hunters.

But unfortunately language is valuable only as the expression of thought. The English word "God" has no particular virtue in itself; it is not more beautiful than other words. Its importance depends altogether upon the meaning which is attached to it. When, therefore, the liberal preacher says that "Jesus is God," the significance of the utterance depends altogether upon what is meant by "God."

And it has already been observed that when the liberal preacher uses the word "God," he means something entirely different from that which the Christian means by the same word. God, at least according to the logical trend of modern liberalism, is not a person separate from the world, but merely the unity that pervades the world. To say, therefore, that Jesus is God means merely that the life of God, which appears in all men, appears with special clearness or richness in Jesus. Such an assertion is diametrically opposed to the Christian belief in the deity of Christ.

Equally opposed to Christian belief is another meaning that is sometimes attached to the assertion that Jesus is God. The word "God" is sometimes used to denote simply the supreme object of men's desires, the highest thing that men know. We have given up the notion, it is said, that there is a Maker and Ruler of the universe; such notions belong to "metaphysics," and are rejected by the modern man. But the word "God," though it can no longer denote the Maker of the universe, is convenient as denoting the object of men's emotions and desires. Of some

men, it can be said that their God is mammon—mammon
is that for which they labor, and to which their hearts are
attached. In a somewhat similar way, the liberal preacher
says that Jesus is God. He does not mean at all to say
that Jesus is identical in nature with a Maker and Ruler
of the universe, of whom an idea could be obtained apart
from Jesus. In such a Being he no longer believes. All
that he means is that the man Jesus—a man here in the
midst of us, and of the same nature as ours—is the highest thing we know. It is obvious that such a way of
thinking is far more widely removed from Christian belief
than is Unitarianism, at least the earlier forms of Unitarianism. For the early Unitarianism no doubt at least
believed in God. The modern liberals, on the other hand,
say that Jesus is God not because they think high of
Jesus, but because they think desperately low of God.

In another way also, liberalism within the "evangelical"
churches is inferior to Unitarianism. It is inferior to
Unitarianism in the matter of honesty. In order to maintain themselves in the evangelical churches and quiet the
fears of their conservative associates, the liberals resort
constantly to a double use of language. A young man,
for example, has received disquieting reports of the unorthodoxy of a prominent preacher. Interrogating the
preacher as to his belief, he receives a reassuring reply.
"You may tell everyone," says the liberal preacher in
effect, "that I believe that Jesus is God." The inquirer
goes away much impressed.

It may well be doubted, however, whether the assertion,
"I believe that Jesus is God," or the like, on the lips of
liberal preachers, is strictly truthful. The liberal
preacher attaches indeed a real meaning to the words, and
that meaning is very dear to his heart. He really does
believe that "Jesus is God." But the trouble is that he

attaches to the words a different meaning from that which
is attached to them by the simple-minded person to whom
he is speaking. He offends, therefore, against the fundamental principle of truthfulness in language. According
to that fundamental principle, language is truthful, not
when the meaning attached to the words by the speaker,
but when the meaning intended to be produced in the mind
of the particular person addressed, is in accordance with
the facts. Thus the truthfulness of the assertion, "I
believe that Jesus is God," depends upon the audience that
is addressed. If the audience is composed of theologically
trained persons, who will attach the same meaning to the
word "God" as that which the speaker attaches to it, then
the language is truthful. But if the audience is composed
of old-fashioned Christians, who have never attached anything but the old meaning to the word "God" (the meaning which appears in the first verse of Genesis), then the
language is untruthful. And in the latter case, not all
the pious motives in the world will make the utterance
right. Christian ethics do not abrogate common honesty:
no possible desire of edifying the Church and of avoiding
offence can excuse a lie.

At any rate, the deity of our Lord, in any real sense of
the word "deity," is of course denied by modern liberalism.
According to the modern liberal Church, Jesus differs
from the rest of men only in degree and not in kind; He
can be divine only if all men are divine. But if the liberal
conception of the deity of Christ thus becomes meaningless, what is the Christian conception? What does the
Christian man mean when he confesses that "Jesus is
God"?

The answer has been given in what has already been
said. It has already been observed that the New Testament represents Jesus as a supernatural Person. But if

Jesus is a supernatural Person He is either divine or else He is an intermediate Being, higher indeed than man, but lower than God. The latter view has been abandoned for many centuries in the Christian Church, and there is not much likelihood that it will be revived; Arianism certainly is dead. The thought of Christ as a super-angelic Being, like God but not God, belongs evidently to pagan mythology, and not to the Bible or to Christian faith. It will usually be admitted, if the theistic conception of the separateness between man and God be held, that Christ is either God or else simply man; He is certainly not a Being intermediate between God and man. If, then, He is not merely man, but a supernatural Person, the conclusion is that He is God.

In the second place, it has already been observed that in the New Testament and in all true Christianity, Jesus is no mere example for faith, but the object of faith. And the faith of which Jesus is the object is clearly religious faith; the Christian man reposes confidence in Jesus in a way that would be out of place in the case of any other than God. It is no lesser thing that is committed to Jesus, but the eternal welfare of the soul. The entire Christian attitude toward Jesus as it is found throughout the New Testament presupposes clearly, then, the deity of our Lord.

It is in the light of this central presupposition that the individual assertions ought to be approached. The individual passages which attest the deity of Christ are not excrescences in the New Testament, but natural fruits of a fundamental conception which is everywhere the same. Those individual passages are not confined to any one book or group of books. In the Pauline Epistles, of course, the passages are particularly plain; the Christ of the Epistles appears again and again as associated only

with the Father and with His Spirit. In the Gospel of
John, also, one does not have to seek very long; the deity
of Christ is almost the theme of the book. But the testimony of the Synoptic Gospels is not really different from
that which appears everywhere else. The way in which
Jesus speaks of *my* Father and *the* Son—for example, in
the famous passage in Matt. xi. 27 (Lk. x. 22): "All
things have been delivered unto me of my Father, and no
man knoweth the Son but the Father, neither knoweth any
man the Father save the Son and He to whomsoever the
Son will reveal Him"—this manner of presenting Jesus'
relation to the Father, absolutely fundamental in the
Synoptic Gospels, involves the assertion of the deity of
our Lord. The Person who so speaks is represented as
being in mysterious union with the eternal God.

Yet the New Testament with equal clearness presents
Jesus as a man. The Gospel of John, which contains at
the beginning the stupendous utterance, "The Word was
God," and dwells constantly upon the deity of the Lord,
also represents Jesus as weary at the well and as thirsty
in the hour of agony on the Cross. Scarcely in the Synoptic Gospels can one discover such drastic touches attesting
the humanity of our Saviour as those which appear again
and again in the Gospel of John. With regard to the
Synoptic Gospels, of course there can be no debate; the
Synoptists clearly present a Person who lived a genuine
human life and was Himself true man.

The truth is, the witness of the New Testament is everywhere the same; the New Testament everywhere presents
One who was both God and man. And it is interesting to
observe how unsuccessful have been all the efforts to reject
one part of this witness and retain the rest. The Apolli-
narians rejected the full humanity of the Lord, but in
doing so they obtained a Person who was very different

from the Jesus of the New Testament. The Jesus of the New Testament was clearly, in the full sense, a man. Others seem to have supposed that the divine and the human were so blended in Jesus that there ⚹⚹ produced a nature neither purely divine nor purely human, but a *tertium quid.* But nothing could be more remote from the New Testament teaching than that. According to the New Testament the divine and human natures were clearly distinct; the divine nature was pure divinity, and the human nature was pure humanity; Jesus was God and man in two *distinct* natures. The Nestorians, on the other hand, so emphasized the distinctness of divine and human in Jesus as to suppose that there were in Jesus two separate persons. But such a Gnosticizing view is plainly contrary to the record; the New Testament plainly teaches the unity of the Person of our Lord.

By elimination of these errors the Church arrived at the New Testament doctrine of two natures in one Person ; the Jesus of the New Testament is "God and man, in two distinct natures, and one Person forever." That doctrine is sometimes regarded as speculative. But nothing could be further from the fact. Whether the doctrine of the two natures is true or false, it was certainly produced not by speculation, but by an attempt to summarize, succinctly and exactly, the Scriptural teaching.

This doctrine is of course rejected by modern liberalism. And it is rejected in a very simple way—by the elimination of the whole higher nature of our Lord. But such radicalism is not a bit more successful than the heresies of the past. The Jesus who is supposed to be left after the elimination of the supernatural element is at best a very shadowy figure; for the elimination of the supernatural logically involves the elimination of much that remains, and the historian constantly approaches the

absurd view which effaces Jesus altogether from the pages
of history.   But even after such dangers have been
avoided, even after the historian, by setting arbitrary
limits to his process of elimination, has succeeded in re-
constructing a purely human Jesus, the Jesus thus constructed is found to be entirely unreal.   He has a moral
contradiction at the very centre of His being—a contradiction due to His Messianic consciousness.   He was pure
and humble and strong and sane, yet He supposed, without basis in fact, that He was to be the final Judge of all
the earth!   The liberal Jesus, despite all the efforts of
modern psychological reconstruction to galvanize Him
into life, remains a manufactured figure of the stage.
Very different is the Jesus of the New Testament and of
the great Scriptural creeds.   That Jesus is indeed mysterious.   Who can fathom the mystery of His Person?
But the mystery is a mystery in which a man can rest.
The Jesus of the New Testament has at least one advantage over the Jesus of modern reconstruction—He is real.
He is not a manufactured figure suitable as a point of
support for ethical maxims, but a genuine Person whom
a man can love.   Men have loved Him through all the
Christian centuries.   And the strange thing is that despite
all the efforts to remove Him from the pages of history,
there are those who love Him still.

CHAPTER VI

It has been observed thus far that liberalism differs from Christianity with regard to the presuppositions of the gospel (the view of God and the view of man), with regard to the Book in which the gospel is contained, and with regard to the Person whose work the gospel sets forth. It is not surprising then that it differs from Christianity in its account of the gospel itself; it is not surprising that it presents an entirely different account of the way of salvation. Liberalism finds salvation (so far as it is willing to speak at all of "salvation") in man; Christianity finds it in an act of God.

The difference with regard to the way of salvation concerns, in the first place, the basis of salvation in the redeeming work of Christ. According to Christian belief, Jesus is our Saviour, not by virtue of what He said, not even by virtue of what He was, but by what He did. He is our Saviour, not because He has inspired us to live the same kind of life that He lived, but because He took upon Himself the dreadful guilt of our sins and bore it instead of us on the cross. Such is the Christian conception of the Cross of Christ. It is ridiculed as being a "subtle theory of the atonement." In reality, it is the plain teaching of the word of God; we know absolutely nothing about an atonement that is not a vicarious atonement, for that is the only atonement of which the New Testament speaks. And this Bible doctrine is not intricate or subtle.

117

On the contrary, though it involves mysteries, it is itself
so simple that a child can understand it. "We deserved
eternal death, but the Lord Jesus, because He loved us,
died instead of us on the cross"—surely there is nothing
so very intricate about that. It is not the Bible doctrine
of the atonement which is difficult to understand—what
are really incomprehensible are the elaborate modern
efforts to get rid of the Bible doctrine in the interests of
human pride.[1]

Modern liberal preachers do indeed sometimes speak
of the "atonement." But they speak of it just as seldom
as they possibly can, and one can see plainly that their
hearts are elsewhere than at the foot of the Cross. Indeed, at this point, as at many others, one has the feeling
that traditional language is being strained to become the
expression of totally alien ideas. And when the traditional phraseology has been stripped away, the essence
of the modern conception of the death of Christ, though
that conception appears in many forms, is fairly plain.
The essence of it is that the death of Christ had an effect
not upon God but only upon man. Sometimes the effect
upon man is conceived of in a very simple way, Christ's
death being regarded merely as an example of self-sacrifice for us to emulate. The uniqueness of this particular
example, then, can be found only in the fact that Christian sentiment, gathering around it, has made it a convenient symbol for all self-sacrifice; it puts in concrete
form what would otherwise have to be expressed in colder
general terms. Sometimes, again, the effect of Christ's
death upon us is conceived of in subtler ways; the death
of Christ, it is said, shows how much God hates sin—since
sin brought even the Holy One to the dreadful Cross—

[1] See "The Second Declaration of the Council on Organic Union,"
in *The Presbyterian*, for March 17, 1921, p. 8.

and we too, therefore, ought to hate sin, as God hates it, and repent. Sometimes, still again, the death of Christ is thought of as displaying the love of God; it exhibits God's own Son as given up for us all. These modern "theories of the atonement" are not all to be placed upon the same plane; the last of them, in particular, may be joined with a high view of Jesus' Person. But they err in that they ignore the dreadful reality of guilt, and make a mere persuasion of the human will all that is needed for salvation. They do indeed all contain an element of truth: it is true that the death of Christ is an example of self-sacrifice which may inspire self-sacrifice in others; it is true that the death of Christ shows how much God hates sin; it is true that the death of Christ displays the love of God. All of these truths are found plainly in the New Testament. But they are swallowed up in a far greater truth—that Christ died instead of us to present us faultless before the throne of God. Without that central truth, all the rest is devoid of real meaning: an example of self-sacrifice is useless to those who are under both the guilt and thralldom of sin; the knowledge of God's hatred of sin can in itself bring only despair; an exhibition of the love of God is a mere display unless there was some underlying reason for the sacrifice. If the Cross is to be restored to its rightful place in Christian life, we shall have to penetrate far beneath the modern theories to Him who loved us and gave Himself for us.

Upon the Christian doctrine of the Cross, modern liberals are never weary of pouring out the vials of their hatred and their scorn. Even at this point, it is true, the hope of avoiding offence is not always abandoned; the words "vicarious atonement" and the like—of course in a sense totally at variance from their Christian meaning— are still sometimes used. But despite such occasional em-

ployment of traditional language the liberal preachers
reveal only too clearly what is in their minds. They speak
with disgust of those who believe "that the blood of our
Lord, shed in a substitutionary death, placates an alienated Deity and makes possible welcome for the returning
sinner." [1] Against the doctrine of the Cross they use
every weapon of caricature and vilification. Thus they
pour out their scorn upon a thing so holy and so precious
that in the presence of it the Christian heart melts in
gratitude too deep for words. It never seems to occur
to modern liberals that in deriding the Christian doctrine
of the Cross, they are trampling upon human hearts.
But the modern liberal attacks upon the Christian doctrine of the Cross may at least serve the purpose of showing what that doctrine is, and from this point of view they
may be examined briefly now.

In the first place, then, the Christian way of salvation
through the Cross of Christ is criticized because it is
dependent upon history. This criticism is sometimes
evaded; it is sometimes said that as Christians we may
attend to what Christ does now for every Christian rather
than to what He did long ago in Palestine. But the
evasion involves a total abandonment of the Christian
faith. If the saving work of Christ were confined to what
He does now for every Christian, there would be no such
thing as a Christian gospel—an account of an event which
put a new face on life. What we should have left would
be simply mysticism, and mysticism is quite different from
Christianity. It is the connection of the present experience of the believer with an actual historic appearance of
Jesus in the world which prevents our religion from being
mysticism and causes it to be Christianity.

[1] Fosdick, *Shall the Fundamentalists Win?*, stenographically re-
ported by Margaret Renton, 1922, p. 5.

It must certainly be admitted, then, that Christianity does depend upon something that happened; our religion must be abandoned altogether unless at a definite point in history Jesus died as a propitiation for the sins of men. Christianity is certainly dependent upon history. But if so, the objection lies very near. Must we really depend for the welfare of our souls upon what happened long ago? Must we really wait until historians have finished disputing about the value of sources and the like before we can have peace with God? Would it not be better to have a salvation which is with us here and now, and which depends only upon what we can see or feel?

With regard to this objection it should be observed that if religion be made independent of history there is no such thing as a gospel. For "gospel" means "good news," tidings, information about something that has happened. A gospel independent of history is a contradiction in terms. The Christian gospel means, not a presentation of what always has been true, but a report of something new—something that imparts a totally different aspect to the situation of mankind. The situation of mankind was desperate because of sin; but God has changed the situation by the atoning death of Christ—that is no mere reflection upon the old, but an account of something new. We are shut up in this world as in a beleaguered camp. To maintain our courage, the liberal preacher offers us exhortation. Make the best of the situation, he says, look on the bright side of life. But unfortunately, such exhortation cannot change the facts. In particular it cannot remove the dreadful fact of sin. Very different is the message of the Christian evangelist. He offers not reflection on the old but tidings of something new, not exhortation but a gospel.[1]

[1] Compare *History and Faith*, 1915, pp. 1-3.

It is true that the Christian gospel is an account, not of something that happened yesterday, but of something that happened long ago; but the important thing is that it really happened. If it really happened, then it makes little difference when it happened. No matter when it happened, whether yesterday or in the first century, it remains a real gospel, a real piece of news.

The happening of long ago, moreover, is in this case confirmed by present experience. The Christian man receives first the account which the New Testament gives of the atoning death of Christ. That account is history. But if true it has effects in the present, and it can be tested by its effects. The Christian man makes trial of the Christian message, and making trial of it he finds it to be true. Experience does not provide a substitute for the documentary evidence, but it does confirm that evidence. The word of the Cross no longer seems to the Christian to be merely a far-off thing, merely a matter to be disputed about by trained theologians. On the contrary, it is received into the Christian's inmost soul, and every day and hour of the Christian's life brings new confirmation of its truth.

In the second place, the Christian doctrine of salvation through the death of Christ is criticized on the ground that it is narrow. It binds salvation to the name of Jesus, and there are many men in the world who have never in any effective way heard of the name of Jesus. What is really needed, we are told, is a salvation which will save all men everywhere, whether they have heard of Jesus or not, and whatever may be the type of life to which they have been reared. Not a new creed, it is said, will meet the universal need of the world, but some means of making effective in right living whatever creed men may chance to have.

This second objection, as well as the first, is sometimes
evaded. It is sometimes said that although one way of
salvation is by means of acceptance of the gospel there
may be other ways. But this method of meeting the objection relinquishes one of the things that are most obviously characteristic of the Christian message—namely,
its exclusiveness. What struck the early observers of
Christianity most forcibly was not merely that salvation
was offered by means of the Christian gospel, but that all
other means were resolutely rejected. The early Christian missionaries demanded an absolutely exclusive devotion to Christ. Such exclusiveness ran directly counter to
the prevailing syncretism of the Hellenistic age. In that
day, many saviours were offered by many religions to the
attention of men, but the various pagan religions could
live together in perfect harmony; when a man became a
devotee of one god, he did not have to give up the others.
But Christianity would have nothing to do with these
"courtly polygamies of the soul"; [1] it demanded an absolutely exclusive devotion; all other Saviours, it insisted,
must be deserted for the one Lord. Salvation, in other
words, was not merely through Christ, but it was only
through Christ. In that little word "only" lay all the
offence. Without that word there would have been no
persecutions; the cultured men of the day would probably
have been willing to give Jesus a place, and an honorable
place, among the saviours of mankind. Without its exclusiveness, the Christian message would have seemed perfectly inoffensive to the men of that day. So modern
liberalism, placing Jesus alongside other benefactors of
mankind, is perfectly inoffensive in the modern world.
All men speak well of it. It is entirely inoffensive. But

[1] Phillimore, in the introduction to his translation of Philostratus,
In Honour of Apollonius of Tyana, 1912, vol. i, p. iii.

it is also entirely futile. The offence of the Cross is done away, but so is the glory and the power.

Thus it must fairly be admitted that Christianity does bind salvation to the name of Christ. The question need not here be discussed whether the benefits of Christ's death are ever applied to those who, though they have come to years of discretion, have not heard or accepted the gospel message. Certainly the New Testament holds out with regard to this matter no clear hope. At the very basis of the work of the apostolic Church is the consciousness of a terrible responsibility. The sole message of life and salvation had been committed to men; that message was at all hazards to be proclaimed while yet there was time. The objection as to the exclusiveness of the Christian way of salvation, therefore, cannot be evaded, but must be met.

In answer to the objection, it may be said simply that the Christian way of salvation is narrow only so long as the Church chooses to let it remain narrow. The name of Jesus is discovered to be strangely adapted to men of every race and of every kind of previous education. And the Church has ample means, with promise of God's Spirit, to bring the name of Jesus to all. If, therefore, this way of salvation is not offered to all, it is not the fault of the way of salvation itself, but the fault of those who fail to use the means that God has placed in their hands.

But, it may be said, is that not a stupendous responsibility to be placed in the hands of weak and sinful men; is it not more natural that God should offer salvation to all without requiring them to accept a new message and thus to be dependent upon the faithfulness of the messengers? The answer to this objection is plain. It is certainly true that the Christian way of salvation places a stupendous responsibility upon men. But that responsibility is like the responsibility which, as ordinary observation shows, God does, as a matter of fact, commit to men. It is like the responsibility, for example, of the parent for the child. The parent has full power to mar the soul as well as the body of the child. The responsibility is terrible; but it is a responsibility which unquestionably exists. Similar is the responsibility of the Church for making the name of Jesus known to all mankind. It is a terrible responsibility; but it exists, and it is just like the other known dealings of God.

But modern liberalism has still more specific objections to the Christian doctrine of the Cross. How can one person, it is asked, suffer for the sins of another? The thing, we are told, is absurd. Guilt, it is said, is personal; if I allow another man to suffer for my fault, my guilt is not thereby one whit diminished.

An answer to this objection is sometimes found in the plain instances in ordinary human life where one person does suffer for another person's sin. In the war, for example, many men died freely for the welfare of others. Here, it is said, we have something analogous to the sacrifice of Christ.

It must be confessed, however, that the analogy is very faint; for it does not touch the specific point at issue. The death of a volunteer soldier in the war was like the death of Christ in that it was a supreme example of self-sacrifice. But the thing to be accomplished by the self-sacrifice was entirely different from the thing which was accomplished on Calvary. The death of those who sacrificed themselves in the war brought peace and protection to the loved ones at home, but it could never avail to wipe out the guilt of sin.

The real answer to the objection is to be found not in the similarity between the death of Christ and other examples of self-sacrifice, but in the profound difference.[1] Why is it that men are no longer willing to trust for their own salvation and for the hope of the world to one act that was done by one Man of long ago? Why is it that they prefer to trust to millions of acts of self-sacrifice wrought by millions of men all through the centuries and in our own day? The answer is plain. It is because men have lost sight of the majesty of Jesus' Person. They think of Him as a man like themselves; and if He was a man like themselves, His death becomes simply an example of self-sacrifice. But there have been millions of examples of self-sacrifice. Why then should we pay such exclusive attention to this one Palestinian example of long ago? Men used to say with reference to Jesus, "There was no other good enough to pay the price of sin." They say so now no longer. On the contrary, every man is now regarded as plenty good enough to pay the price of sin if, whether in peace or in war, he will only go bravely over the top in some noble cause.

It is perfectly true that no mere man can pay the penalty of another man's sin. But it does not follow that Jesus could not do it; for Jesus was no mere man but the eternal Son of God. Jesus is master of the innermost secrets of the moral world. He has done what none other could possibly do; He has borne our sin.

The Christian doctrine of the atonement, therefore, is altogether rooted in the Christian doctrine of the deity of Christ. The reality of an atonement for sin depends altogether upon the New Testament presentation of the Person of Christ. And even the hymns dealing with the Cross which we sing in Church can be placed in an ascend-

---

[1] For what follows, compare "The Church in the War," in *The Presbyterian*, for May 29, 1919, pp. 10f.

ing scale according as they are based upon a lower or a higher view of Jesus' Person. At the very bottom of the scale is that familiar hymn:

> Nearer, my God, to thee,
> Nearer to thee!
> E'en though it be a cross
> That raiseth me.

That is a perfectly good hymn. It means that our trials may be a discipline to bring us nearer to God. The thought is not opposed to Christianity; it is found in the New Testament. But many persons have the impression, because the word "cross" is found in the hymn, that there is something specifically Christian about it, and that it has something to do with the gospel. This impression is entirely false. In reality, the cross that is spoken of is not the Cross of Christ, but our own cross; the verse simply means that our own crosses or trials may be a means to bring us nearer to God. It is a perfectly good thought, but certainly it is not the gospel. One can only be sorry that the people on the *Titanic* could not find a better hymn to use in the last solemn hour of their lives.

But there is another hymn in the hymn-book:

> In the cross of Christ I glory,
> Towering o'er the wrecks of time;
> All the light of sacred story
> Gathers round its head sublime.

That is certainly better. It is here not our own crosses but the Cross of Christ, the actual event that took place on Calvary, that is spoken of, and that event is celebrated as the centre of all history. Certainly the Christian man can sing that hymn. But one misses even there the full Christian sense of the meaning of the Cross; the Cross is celebrated, but it is not understood.

It is well, therefore, that there is another hymn in our hymn-book:

> When I survey the wondrous cross
> On which the Prince of glory died,
> My richest gain I count but loss,
> And pour contempt on all my pride.

There at length are heard the accents of true Christian feeling—"the wondrous cross on which the Prince of glory died." When we come to see that it was no mere man who suffered on Calvary but the Lord of Glory, then we shall be willing to say that one drop of the precious blood of Jesus is of more value, for our own salvation and for the hope of society, than all the rivers of blood that have flowed upon the battlefields of history.

Thus the objection to the vicarious sacrifice of Christ disappears altogether before the tremendous Christian sense of the majesty of Jesus' Person. It is perfectly true that the Christ of modern naturalistic reconstruction never could have suffered for the sins of others; but it is very different in the case of the Lord of Glory. And if the notion of vicarious atonement be so absurd as modern opposition would lead us to believe, what shall be said of the Christian experience that has been based upon it? The modern liberal Church is fond of appealing to experience. But where shall true Christian experience be found if not in the blessed peace which comes from Calvary? That peace comes only when a man recognizes that all his striving to be right with God, all his feverish endeavor to keep the Law before he can be saved, is unnecessary, and that the Lord Jesus has wiped out the handwriting that was against him by dying instead of him on the Cross. Who can measure the depth of the peace and joy that comes from this blessed knowledge? Is it a "theory of the atonement," a delusion of man's fancy? Or is it the very truth of God?

But still another objection remains against the Christian doctrine of the Cross. The objection concerns the character of God. What a degraded view of God it is, the modern liberal exclaims, when God is represented as being "alienated" from man, and as waiting coldly until a price be paid before He grants salvation! In reality, we are told, God is more willing to forgive sin than we are willing to be forgiven; reconciliation, therefore, can have to do only with man; it all depends upon us; God will receive us any time we choose.

The objection depends of course upon the liberal view of sin. If sin is so trifling a matter as the liberal Church supposes, then indeed the curse of God's law can be taken very lightly, and God can easily let by-gones be by-gones.

This business of letting by-gones be by-gones has a pleasant sound. But in reality it is the most heartless thing in the world. It will not do at all even in the case of sins committed against our fellow-men. To say nothing of sin against God, what shall be done about the harm that we have wrought to our neighbor? Sometimes, no doubt, the harm can be repaired. If we have defrauded our neighbor of a sum of money, we can pay the sum back with interest. But in the case of the more serious wrongs such repayment is usually quite impossible. The more serious wrongs are those that are done, not to the bodies, but to the souls of men. And who can think with complacency of wrongs of that kind which he has committed? Who can bear to think, for example, of the harm that he has done to those younger than himself by a bad example? And what of those sad words, spoken to those we love, that have left scars never to be obliterated by the hand of time? In the presence of such memories, we are told by

the modern preacher simply to repent and to let by-gones
be by-gones. But what a heartless thing is such repentance! *We* escape into some higher, happier, respectable
life. But what of those whom we by our example and by
our words have helped to drag down to the brink of hell?
We forget them and let by-gones be by-gones!

Such repentance will never wipe out the guilt of sin—
not even sin committed against our fellow-men, to say
nothing of sin against our God. The truly penitent man
longs to wipe out the effects of sin, not merely to forget
sin. But who can wipe out the effects of sin? Others are
suffering because of our past sins; and we can attain no
real peace until we suffer in their stead. We long to go
back into the tangle of our life, and make right the things
that are wrong—at least to suffer where we have caused
others to suffer. And something like that Christ did for
us when He died instead of us on the cross; He atoned for
all our sins.

The sorrow for sins committed against one's fellow-
men does indeed remain in the Christian's heart. And he
will seek by every means that is within his power to repair
the damage that he has done. But atonement at least has
been made—made as truly as if the sinner himself had
suffered with and for those whom he has wronged. And
the sinner himself, by a mystery of grace, becomes right
with God. All sin at bottom is a sin against God.
"Against thee, thee only have I sinned" is the cry of a
true penitent. How terrible is the sin against God! Who
can recall the wasted moments and years? Gone they are,
never to return; gone the little allotted span of life; gone
the little day in which a man must work. Who can measure the irrevocable guilt of a wasted life? Yet even for
such guilt God has provided a fountain of cleansing in the
precious blood of Christ. God has clothed us with Christ's

righteousness as with a garment; in Christ we stand spotless before the judgment throne.

Thus to deny the necessity of atonement is to deny the existence of a real moral order. And it is strange how those who venture upon such denial can regard themselves as disciples of Jesus; for if one thing is clear in the record of Jesus' life it is that Jesus recognized the justice, as distinguished from the love, of God. God is love, according to Jesus, but He is not only love; Jesus spoke, in terrible words, of the sin that shall never be forgiven either in this world or in that which is to come. Clearly Jesus recognized the existence of retributive justice; Jesus was far from accepting the light modern view of sin.

But what, then, it will be objected, becomes of God's love? Even if it be admitted that justice demands punishment for sin, the modern liberal theologian will say, what becomes of the Christian doctrine that justice is swallowed up by grace? If God is represented as waiting for a price to be paid before sin shall be forgiven, perhaps His justice may be rescued, but what becomes of His love?

Modern liberal teachers are never tired of ringing the changes upon this objection. They speak with horror of the doctrine of an "alienated" or an "angry" God. In answer, of course it would be easy to point to the New Testament. The New Testament clearly speaks of the wrath of God and the wrath of Jesus Himself; and all the teaching of Jesus presupposes a divine indignation against sin. With what possible right, then, can those who reject this vital element in Jesus' teaching and example regard themselves as true disciples of His? The truth is that the modern rejection of the doctrine of God's wrath proceeds from a light view of sin which is totally at variance with the teaching of the whole New Testament and of Jesus Himself. If a man has once come under a

true conviction of sin, he will have little difficulty with
the doctrine of the Cross.

But as a matter of fact the modern objection to the
doctrine of the atonement on the ground that that doctrine is contrary to the love of God, is based upon the
most abysmal misunderstanding of the doctrine itself.
The modern liberal teachers persist in speaking of the
sacrifice of Christ as though it were a sacrifice made by
some one other than God. They speak of it as though it
meant that God waits coldly until a price is paid to Him
before He forgives sin. As a matter of fact, it means
nothing of the kind; the objection ignores that which is
absolutely fundamental in the Christian doctrine of the
Cross. The fundamental thing is that God Himself, and
not another, makes the sacrifice for sin—God Himself in
the person of the Son who assumed our nature and died
for us, God Himself in the Person of the Father who
spared not His own Son but offered Him up for us all.
Salvation is as free *for us* as the air we breathe; God's
the dreadful cost, ours the gain. "God so loved the world
that He gave His only begotten Son." Such love is very
different from the complacency found in the God of modern preaching; this love is love that did not count the
cost; it is love that is love indeed.

This love and this love alone brings true joy to men.
Joy is indeed being sought by the modern liberal Church.
But it is being sought in ways that are false. How may
communion with God be made joyful? Obviously, we are
told, by emphasizing the comforting attributes of God—
His long-suffering, His love. Let us, it is urged, regard
Him not as a moody Despot, not as a sternly righteous
Judge, but simply as a loving Father. Away with the
horrors of the old theology! Let us worship a God in
whom we can rejoice.

Two questions arise with regard to this method of making religion joyful—in the first place, Does it work? and in the second place, Is it true?

Does it work? It certainly ought to work. How can anyone be unhappy when the ruler of the universe is declared to be the loving Father of all men who will never permanently inflict pain upon His children? Where is the sting of remorse if all sin will necessarily be forgiven? Yet men are strangely ungrateful. After the modern preacher has done his part with all diligence—after everything unpleasant has carefully been eliminated from the conception of God, after His unlimited love has been celebrated with the eloquence that it deserves—the congregation somehow persistently refuses to burst into the old ecstasies of joy. The truth is, the God of modern preaching, though He may perhaps be very good, is rather uninteresting. Nothing is so insipid as indiscriminate good humor. Is that really love that costs so little? If God will necessarily forgive, no matter what we do, why trouble ourselves about Him at all? Such a God may deliver us from the fear of hell. But His heaven, if He has any, is full of sin.

The other objection to the modern encouraging idea of God is that it is not true. How do you know that God is all love and kindness? Surely not through nature, for it is full of horrors. Human suffering may be unpleasant, but it is real, and God must have something to do with it. Just as surely not through the Bible. For it was from the Bible that the old theologians derived that conception of God which you would reject as gloomy. "The Lord thy God," the Bible says, "is a consuming fire." Or is Jesus alone your authority? You are no better off. For it was Jesus who spoke of the outer darkness and the everlasting fire, of the sin that shall not be forgiven either in this age or in that which is to come. Or do you appeal, for your comforting idea of God, to a twentieth-century revelation granted immediately to you? It is to be feared that you will convince no one but yourself.

Religion cannot be made joyful simply by looking on the bright side of God. For a one-sided God is not a real God, and it is the real God alone who can satisfy the longing of our soul. God is love, but is He only love? God is love, but is love God? Seek joy alone, then, seek joy at any cost, and you will not find it. How then may it be attained?

The search for joy in religion seems to have ended in disaster. God is found to be enveloped in impenetrable mystery, and in awful righteousness; man is confined in the prison of the world, trying to make the best of his condition, beautifying the prison with tinsel, yet secretly dissatisfied with his bondage, dissatisfied with a merely relative goodness which is no goodness at all, dissatisfied with the companionship of his sinful fellows, unable to forget his heavenly destiny and his heavenly duty, longing for communion with the Holy One. There seems to be no hope; God is separate from sinners; there is no room for joy, but only a certain fearful looking for of judgment and fiery indignation.

Yet such a God has at least one advantage over the comforting God of modern preaching—He is alive, He is sovereign, He is not bound by His creation or by His creatures, He can perform wonders. Could He even save us if He would? He has saved us—in that message the gospel consists. It could not have been foretold; still less could the manner of it have been foretold. That Birth, that Life, that Death—why was it done just thus and then and there? It all seems so very local, so very particular, so very unphilosophical, so very unlike what might

have been expected. Are not our own methods of salvation, men say, better than that? "Are not Abana and
Pharpar, rivers of Damascus, better than all the waters of
Israel?" Yet what if it were true? "So, the All-Great
were the All-Loving too"—God's own Son delivered up for
us all, freedom from the world, sought by philosophers of
all the ages, offered now freely to every simple soul, things
hidden from the wise and prudent revealed unto babes, the
long striving over, the impossible accomplished, sin conquered by mysterious grace, communion at length with the
holy God, our Father which art in heaven!

Surely this and this alone is joy. But it is a joy that is
akin to fear. It is a fearful thing to fall into the hands
of the living God. Were we not safer with a God of our
own devising—love and only love, a Father and nothing
else, one before whom we could stand in our own merit
without fear? He who will may be satisfied with such a
God. But we, God help us—sinful as we are, we would
see Jehovah. Despairing, hoping, trembling, half-doubt-
ing and half-believing, trusting all to Jesus, we venture
into the presence of the very God. And in His presence
we live.

The atoning death of Christ, and that alone, has presented sinners as righteous in God's sight; the Lord Jesus
has paid the full penalty of their sins, and clothed them
with His perfect righteousness before the judgment seat
of God. But Christ has done for Christians even far more
than that. He has given to them not only a new and
right relation to God, but a new life in God's presence for
evermore. He has saved them from the power as well as
from the guilt of sin. The New Testament does not end
with the death of Christ; it does not end with the triumphant words of Jesus on the Cross, "It is finished." The
death was followed by the resurrection, and the resurrec-

tion like the death was for our sakes. Jesus rose from the dead into a new life of glory and power, and into that life He brings those for whom He died. The Christian, on the basis of Christ's redeeming work, not only has died unto sin, but also lives unto God.

Thus was completed the redeeming work of Christ—the work for which He entered into the world. The account of that work is the "gospel," the "good news." It never could have been predicted, for sin deserves naught but eternal death. But God triumphed over sin through the grace of our Lord Jesus Christ.

But how is the redeeming work of Christ applied to the individual Christian man? The answer of the New Testament is plain. According to the New Testament the work of Christ is applied to the individual Christian man by the Holy Spirit. And this work of the Holy Spirit is part of the creative work of God. It is not accomplished by the ordinary use of means; it is not accomplished merely by using the good that is already in man. On the contrary, it is something new. It is not an influence upon the life, but the beginning of a new life; it is not development of what we had already, but a new birth. At the very centre of Christianity are the words, "Ye must be born again."

These words are despised to-day. They involve supernaturalism, and the modern man is opposed to supernaturalism in the experience of the individual as much as in the realm of history. A cardinal doctrine of modern liberalism is that the world's evil may be overcome by the world's good; no help is thought to be needed from outside the world.

This doctrine is propagated in various ways. It runs all through the popular literature of our time. It dominates religious literature, and it appears even upon the stage. Some years ago great popularity was attained by a play which taught the doctrine in powerful fashion. The play began with a scene in a London boarding-house. And it was a very discouraging scene. The persons in that boarding-house were not by any means desperate criminals, but one could almost have wished that they had been —they would have been so much more interesting. As it was, they were simply sordid, selfish persons, snapping and snarling about things to eat and about creature comforts—the sort of persons about whom one is tempted to say that they have no souls. The scene was a powerful picture of the hideousness of the commonplace. But presently the mysterious stranger of "the third floor back" entered upon the scene, and all was changed. He had no creed to offer, and no religion. But he simply engaged in conversation with everyone in that boarding-house, and discovered the one good point in every individual life. Somewhere in every life there was some one good thing—some one true human affection, some one noble ambition. It had long been hidden by a thick coating of sordidness and selfishness; its very existence had been forgotten. But it was there, and when it was brought to the light the whole life was transformed. Thus the evil that was in man was overcome by the good that was already there.

The same thing is taught in more immediately practical ways. For example, there are those who would apply it to the prisoners in our jails. The inmates of jails and penitentiaries constitute no doubt unpromising material. But it is a great mistake, it is said, to tell them that they are bad, to discourage them by insisting upon their sin. On the contrary, we are told, what ought to be done is to find the good that is already in them and build upon that; we ought to appeal to some latent sense of honor which shows that even criminals possess the remnants of our

common human nature. Thus again the evil that is in
man is to be overcome not by a foreign good but by a good
which man himself possesses.

Certainly there is a large element of truth in this modern principle. That element of truth is found in the
Bible. The Bible does certainly teach that the good that
is already in man ought to be fostered in order to check
the evil. Whatsoever things are true and pure and of
good report—we ought to think on those things. Certainly the principle of overcoming the world's evil by the
good already in the world is a great principle. The old
theologians recognized it to the full in their doctrine of
"common grace." There is something in the world even
apart from Christianity which restrains the worst manifestations of evil. And that something ought to be used.
Without the use of it, this world could not be lived in for
a day. The use of it is certainly a great principle; it will
certainly accomplish many useful things.

But there is one thing which it will not accomplish. It
will not remove the disease of sin. It will indeed palliate
the symptoms of the disease; it will change the form of the
disease. Sometimes the disease is hidden, and there are
those who think that it is cured. But then it bursts forth
in some new way, as in 1914, and startles the world. What
is really needed is not a salve to palliate the symptoms of
sin, but a remedy that attacks the root of the disease.

In reality, however, the figure of disease is misleading.
The only true figure—if indeed it can be called merely a
figure—is the one which is used in the Bible. Man is not
merely ill, but he is dead, in trespasses and sins, and what
is really needed is a new life. That life is given by the
Holy Spirit in "regeneration" or the new birth.

Many are the passages and many are the ways in which
the central doctrine of the new birth is taught in the Word

of God. One of the most stupendous passages is Gal.
ii. 20: "I have been crucified with Christ; and it is no
longer I that live but Christ liveth in me." That passage
was called by Bengel the marrow of Christianity. And it
was rightly so called. It refers to the objective basis of
Christianity in the redeeming work of Christ, and it contains also the supernaturalism of Christian experience.
"It is no longer I that live, but Christ liveth in me"—these
are extraordinary words. "If you look upon Christians,"
Paul says in effect, "you see so many manifestations of the
life of Christ." Undoubtedly if the words of Gal. ii. 20
stood alone they might be taken in a mystical or pantheistic sense; they might be taken to involve the merging
of the personality of the Christian in the personality of
Christ. But Paul had no reason to fear such a misinter-
pretation, for he had fortified himself against it by the
whole of his teaching. The new relation of the Christian
to Christ, according to Paul, involves no loss of the separate personality of the Christian; on the contrary, it is
everywhere intensely personal; it is not a merely mystical
relationship to the All or the Absolute, but a relationship
of love existing between one person and another. Just
because Paul had fortified himself against misunderstanding, he was not afraid of an extreme boldness of language.
"It is no longer I that live, but Christ liveth in me"—these
words involve a tremendous conception of the break that
comes in a man's life when he becomes a Christian. It is
almost as though he became a new person—so stupendous
is the change. These words were not written by a man
who believed that Christianity means merely the entrance
of a new motive into the life; Paul believed with all his
mind and heart in the doctrine of the new creation or the
new birth.

That doctrine represents one aspect of the salvation

which was wrought by Christ and is applied by His Spirit. But there is another aspect of the same salvation. Regeneration means a new life; but there is also a new relation in which the believer stands toward God. That new relation is instituted by "justification"—the act of God by which a sinner is pronounced righteous in His sight because of the atoning death of Christ. It is not necessary to ask whether justification comes before regeneration or *vice versa;* in reality they are two aspects of one salvation. And they both stand at the very beginning of the Christian life. The Christian has not merely the promise of a new life, but he has already a new life. And he has not merely the promise of being pronounced righteous in God's sight (though the blessed pronouncement will be confirmed on the judgment day), but he is already pronounced righteous here and now. At the beginning of every Christian life there stands, not a process, but a definite act of God.

That does not mean that every Christian can tell exactly at what moment he was justified and born again. Some Christians, indeed, are really able to give day and hour of their conversion. It is a grievous sin to ridicule the experience of such men. Sometimes, indeed, they are inclined to ignore the steps in the providence of God which prepared for the great change. But they are right on the main point. They know that when on such and such a day they kneeled in prayer they were still in their sins, and when they rose from their knees they were children of God never to be separated from Him. Such experience is a very holy thing. But on the other hand it is a mistake to demand that it should be universal. There are Christians who can give day and hour of their conversion, but the great majority do not know exactly at what moment they were saved. The effects of the act are plain, but the act itself was done in the quietness of God. Such, very often, is the experience of children brought up by Christian parents. It is not necessary that all should pass through agonies of soul before being saved; there are those to whom faith comes peacefully and easily through the nurture of Christian homes. But however it be manifested, the beginning of the Christian life is an act of God. It is an act of God and not an act of man.

That does not mean, however, that in the beginning of the Christian life God deals with us as with sticks or stones, unable to understand what is being done. On the contrary He deals with us as with persons; salvation has a place in the conscious life of man; God uses in our salvation a conscious act of the human soul—an act which though it is itself the work of God's Spirit, is at the same time an act of man. That act of man which God produces and employs in salvation is faith. At the centre of Christianity is the doctrine of "justification by faith."

In exalting faith, we are not immediately putting ourselves in contradiction to modern thought. Indeed faith is being exalted very high by men of the most modern type. But what kind of faith? There emerges the difference of opinion.

Faith is being exalted so high to-day that men are being satisfied with any kind of faith, just so it is faith. It makes no difference what is believed, we are told, just so the blessed attitude of faith is there. The undogmatic faith, it is said, is better than the dogmatic, because it is purer faith—faith less weakened by the alloy of knowledge.

Now it is perfectly clear that such employment of faith merely as a beneficent state of the soul is bringing some results. Faith in the most absurd things sometimes pro-

duces the most beneficent and far-reaching results. But
the disturbing thing is that all faith has an object. The
scientific observer may not think that it is the object that
does the work; from his vantage point he may see clearly
that it is really the faith, considered simply as a psychological phenomenon, that is the important thing, and that
any other object would have answered as well. But the
one who does the believing is always convinced just exactly
that it is not the faith, but the object of the faith, which
is helping him. The moment he becomes convinced that it
is merely the faith that is helping him, the faith disappears; for faith always involves a conviction of the objective truth or trustworthiness of the object. If the object
is not really trustworthy then the faith is a false faith.
It is perfectly true that such a false faith will often help
a man. Things that are false will accomplish a great
many useful things in the world. If I take a counterfeit
coin and buy a dinner with it, the dinner is every bit as
good as if the coin were a product of the mint. And what
a very useful thing a dinner is! But just as I am on my
way downtown to buy a dinner for a poor man, an expert
tells me that my coin is a counterfeit. The miserable,
heartless theorizer! While he is going into uninteresting,
learned details about the primitive history of that coin, a
poor man is dying for want of bread. So it is with faith.
Faith is so very useful, they tell us, that we must not
scrutinize its basis in truth. But, the great trouble is,
such an avoidance of scrutiny itself involves the destruction of faith. For faith is essentially dogmatic. Despite
all you can do, you cannot remove the element of intellectual assent from it. Faith is the opinion that some person
will do something for you. If that person really will do
that thing for you, then the faith is true. If he will not
do it, then the faith is false. In the latter case, not all

the benefits in the world will make the faith true. Though it has transformed the world from darkness to light, though it has produced thousands of glorious healthy lives, it remains a pathological phenomenon. It is false, and sooner or later it is sure to be found out.

Such counterfeits should be removed, not out of a love of destruction, but in order to leave room for the pure gold, the existence of which is implied in the presence of the counterfeits. Faith is often based upon error, but there would be no faith at all unless it were sometimes based upon truth. But if Christian faith is based upon truth, then it is not the faith which saves the Christian but the object of the faith. And the object of the faith is Christ. Faith, then, according to the Christian view, means simply receiving a gift. To have faith in Christ means to cease trying to win God's favor by one's own character; the man who believes in Christ simply accepts the sacrifice which Christ offered on Calvary. The result of such faith is a new life and all good works; but the salvation itself is an absolutely free gift of God.

Very different is the conception of faith which prevails in the liberal Church. According to modern liberalism, faith is essentially the same as "making Christ Master" in one's life; at least it is by making Christ Master in the life that the welfare of men is sought. But that simply means that salvation is thought to be obtained by our own obedience to the commands of Christ. Such teaching is just a sublimated form of legalism. Not the sacrifice of Christ, on this view, but our own obedience to God's law, is the ground of hope.

In this way the whole achievement of the Reformation has been given up, and there has been a return to the religion of the Middle Ages. At the beginning of the sixteenth century, God raised up a man who began to read the Epistle to the Galatians with his own eyes. The result was the rediscovery of the doctrine of justification by faith. Upon that rediscovery has been based the whole of our evangelical freedom. As expounded by Luther and Calvin the Epistle to the Galatians became the "Magna Charta of Christian liberty." But modern liberalism has returned to the old interpretation of Galatians which was urged against the Reformers. Thus Professor Burton's elaborate commentary on the Epistle, despite all its extremely valuable modern scholarship, is in one respect a mediæval book; it has returned to an anti-Reformation exegesis, by which Paul is thought to be attacking in the Epistle only the piecemeal morality of the Pharisees. In reality, of course, the object of Paul's attack is the thought that in any way man can earn his acceptance with God. What Paul is primarily interested in is not spiritual religion over against ceremonialism, but the free grace of God over against human merit.

The grace of God is rejected by modern liberalism. And the result is slavery—the slavery of the law, the wretched bondage by which man undertakes the impossible task of establishing his own righteousness as a ground of acceptance with God. It may seem strange at first sight that "liberalism," of which the very name means freedom, should in reality be wretched slavery. But the phenomenon is not really so strange. Emancipation from the blessed will of God always involves bondage to some worse taskmaster.

Thus it may be said of the modern liberal Church, as of the Jerusalem of Paul's day, that "she is in bondage with her children." God grant that she may turn again to the liberty of the gospel of Christ!

The liberty of the gospel depends upon the gift of God by which the Christian life is begun—a gift which involves justification, or the removal of the guilt of sin and the establishment of a right relation between the believer and God, and regeneration or the new birth, which makes of the Christian man a new creature.

But there is one obvious objection to this high doctrine, and the objection leads on to a fuller account of the Christian way of salvation. The obvious objection to the doctrine of the new creation is that it does not seem to be in accord with the observed fact. Are Christians really new creatures? It certainly does not seem so. They are subject to the same old conditions of life to which they were subject before; if you look upon them you cannot notice any very obvious change. They have the same weaknesses, and, unfortunately, they have sometimes the same sins. The new creation, if it be really new, does not seem to be very perfect; God can hardly look upon it and say, as of the first creation, that it is all very good.

This is a very real objection. But Paul meets it gloriously in the very same verse, already considered, in which the doctrine of the new creation is so boldly proclaimed. "It is no longer I that live, but Christ liveth in me"—that is the doctrine of the new creation. But immediately the objection is taken up; "The life which I now live in the flesh," Paul continues, "I live by the faith which is in the Son of God who loved me and gave Himself for me." "The life which I now live in the flesh"—there is the admission. Paul admits that the Christian does live a life in the flesh, subject to the same old earthly conditions and with a continued battle against sin. "But," says Paul (and here the objection is answered), "the life which I now live in the flesh I live by the faith which is in the Son of God who loved me and gave Himself for me." The Christian life is lived by faith and not by sight; the great change has not yet come to full fruition; sin has not yet been fully conquered; the beginning of the Christian life is a new *birth*, not an immediate creation of the full-grown man. But although the new life has not yet come to full fruition, the Christian knows that the fruition will not fail; he is confident that the God who has begun a good work in him will complete it unto the day of Christ; he knows that the Christ who has loved him and given Himself for him will not fail him now, but through the Holy Spirit will build him up unto the perfect man. That is what Paul means by living the Christian life by faith.

Thus the Christian life, though it begins by a momentary act of God, is continued by a process. In other words—to use theological language—justification and regeneration are followed by sanctification. In principle the Christian is already free from the present evil world, but in practice freedom must still be attained. Thus the Christian life is not a life of idleness, but a battle.

That is what Paul means when he speaks of faith working through love (Gal. v. 6). The faith that he makes the means of salvation is not an idle faith, like the faith which is condemned in the Epistle of James, but a faith that works. The work that it performs is love, and what love is Paul explains in the last section of the Epistle to the Galatians. Love, in the Christian sense, is not a mere emotion, but a very practical and a very comprehensive thing. It involves nothing less than the keeping of the whole law of God. "The whole law is fulfilled in one word, even in this: Thou shalt love thy neighbor as thyself." Yet the practical results of faith do not mean that faith itself is a work. It is a significant thing that in that last "practical" section of Galatians Paul does not say that faith produces the life of love; he says that the Spirit of God produces it. The Spirit, then, in that section is represented as doing exactly what in the pregnant words, "faith working through love," is attributed to faith. The apparent contradiction simply leads to the true conception of faith. True faith does not do anything. When it is said to do something (for example, when we say that it can remove mountains), that is only by a very natural shortness of expression. Faith is the exact opposite of works; faith does not give, it receives. So when Paul says that we do something by faith, that is just another way of saying that of ourselves we do nothing; when it is said that faith works through love that means that through faith the necessary basis of all Christian work has been obtained in the removal of guilt and the birth of the new man, and that the Spirit of God has been received —the Spirit who works with and through the Christian man for holy living. The force which enters the Christian life through faith and works itself out through love is the power of the Spirit of God.

But the Christian life is lived not only by faith, it is also lived in hope. The Christian is in the midst of a sore battle. And as for the condition of the world at large— nothing but the coldest heartlessness could be satisfied with that. It is certainly true that the whole creation groaneth and travaileth in pain together until now. Even in the Christian life there are things that we should like to see removed; there are fears within as well as fightings without; even within the Christian life there are sad evidences of sin. But according to the hope which Christ has given us, there will be final victory, and the struggle of this world will be followed by the glories of heaven. That hope runs all through the Christian life; Christianity is not engrossed by this transitory world, but measures all things by the thought of eternity.

But at this point an objection is frequently raised. The "otherworldliness" of Christianity is objected to as a form of selfishness. The Christian, it is said, does what is right because of the hope of heaven, but how much nobler is the man who because of duty walks boldly into the darkness of annihilation!

The objection would have some weight if heaven according to Christian belief were mere enjoyment. But as a matter of fact heaven is communion with God and with His Christ. It can be said reverently that the Christian longs for heaven not only for his own sake, but also for the sake of God. Our present love is so cold, our present service so weak; and we would one day love and serve Him as His love deserves. It is perfectly true that the Christian is dissatisfied with the present world, but it is a holy dissatisfaction; it is that hunger and thirst after righteousness which our Saviour blessed. We are separated from the Saviour now by the veil of sense and by the effects of sin, and it is not selfish to long to see Him face to face. To relinquish such longing is not unselfishness, but is like the cold heartlessness of a man who could part from father or mother or wife or child without a pang. It is not selfish to long for the One whom not having seen we love.

Such is the Christian life—it is a life of conflict, but it is also a life of hope. It views this world under the aspect of eternity; the fashion of this world passeth away, and all must stand before the judgment seat of Christ.

Very different is the "program" of the modern liberal Church. In that program, heaven has little place, and this world is really all in all. The rejection of the Christian hope is not always definite or conscious; sometimes the liberal preacher tries to maintain a belief in the immortality of the soul. But the real basis of the belief in immortality has been given up by the rejection of the New Testament account of the resurrection of Christ.

And, practically, the liberal preacher has very little to
say about the other world. This world is really the centre
of all his thoughts; religion itself, and even God, are made
merely a means for the betterment of conditions upon this
earth. Thus religion has become a mere function of the community or of the state. So it is looked upon by the men
of the present day. Even hard-headed business men and
politicians have become convinced that religion is needed.
But it is thought to be needed merely as a means to an
end. We have tried to get along without religion, it is
said, but the experiment was a failure, and now religion
must be called in to help.

For example, there is the problem of the immigrants;
great populations have found a place in our country;
they do not speak our language or know our customs;
and we do not know what to do with them. We have
attacked them by oppressive legislation or proposals of
legislation, but such measures have not been altogether
effective. Somehow these people display a perverse at-
tachment to the language that they learned at their
mother's knee. It may be strange that a man should love
the language that he learned at his mother's knee, but
these people do love it, and we are perplexed in our efforts
to produce a unified American people. So religion is
called in to help; we are inclined to proceed against the
immigrants now with a Bible in one hand and a club in the
other offering them the blessings of liberty. That is what
is sometimes meant by "Christian Americanization."

Another puzzling problem is the problem of industrial
relations. Self-interest has here been appealed to; em-
ployers and employees have had pointed out to them the
plain commercial advantages of conciliation. But all to
no purpose. Class clashes still against class in the de-

structiveness of industrial warfare. And sometimes **false**
doctrine provides a basis for false practice; the danger
of Bolshevism is ever in the air. Here again repressive
measures have been tried without avail; the freedom of
speech and of the press has been radically curtailed.
But repressive legislation seems unable to check the march
of ideas. Perhaps, therefore, in these matters also, religion must be invoked.

Still another problem faces the modern world—the
problem of international peace. This problem also seemed
at one time nearly solved; self-interest seemed likely to
be sufficient; there were many who supposed that the
bankers would prevent another European war. But all
such hopes were cruelly shattered in 1914, and there is
not a whit of evidence that they are better founded now
than they were then. Here again, therefore, self-interest
is insufficient; and religion must be called in to help.

Such considerations have led to a renewed public interest in the subject of religion; religion is discovered after
all to be a useful thing. But the trouble is that in being
utilized religion is also being degraded and destroyed.
Religion is being regarded more and more as a mere means
to a higher end.[1] The change can be detected with especial
clearness in the way in which missionaries commend their
cause. Fifty years ago, missionaries made their appeal
in the light of eternity. "Millions of men," they were
accustomed to say, "are going down to eternal destruction; Jesus is a Saviour sufficient for all; send us out
therefore with the message of salvation while yet there is

[1] For a penetrating criticism of this tendency, especially as it
would result in the control of religious education by the community,
and for an eloquent advocacy of the opposite view, which makes
Christianity an end in itself, see Harold McA. Robinson, "Democracy
and Christianity," in *The Christian Educator*, Vol. V, No. 1, for
October, 1920, pp. 3-5.

time." Some missionaries, thank God, still speak in that way. But very many missionaries make quite a different appeal. "We are missionaries to India," they say. "Now India is in ferment; Bolshevism is creeping in; send us out to India that the menace may be checked." Or else they say: "We are missionaries to Japan; Japan will be dominated by militarism unless the principles of Jesus have sway; send us out therefore to prevent the calamity of war."

The same great change appears in community life. A new community, let us say, has been formed. It possesses many things that naturally belong to a well-ordered community; it has a drug-store, and a country club, and a school. "But there is one thing," its inhabitants say to themselves, "that is still lacking; we have no church. But a church is a recognized and necessary part of every healthy community. We must therefore have a church." And so an expert in community church-building is summoned to take the necessary steps. The persons who speak in this way usually have little interest in religion for its own sake; it has never occurred to them to enter into the secret place of communion with the holy God. But religion is thought to be necessary for a healthy community; and therefore for the sake of the community they are willing to have a church.

Whatever may be thought of this attitude toward religion, it is perfectly plain that the *Christian* religion cannot be treated in any such way. The moment it is so treated it ceases to be Christian. For if one thing is plain it is that Christianity refuses to be regarded as a mere means to a higher end. Our Lord made that perfectly clear when He said: "If any man come to me, and hate not his father and mother . . . he cannot be my disciple" (Luke xiv. 26). Whatever else those stupendous words may mean, they certainly mean that the relationship to Christ takes precedence of all other relationships, even the holiest of relationships like those that exist between husband and wife and parent and child. Those other relationships exist for the sake of Christianity and not Christianity for the sake of them. Christianity will indeed accomplish many useful things in this world, but if it is accepted in order to accomplish those useful things it is not Christianity. Christianity will combat Bolshevism; but if it is accepted in order to combat Bolshevism, it is not Christianity: Christianity will produce a unified nation, in a slow but satisfactory way; but if it is accepted in order to produce a unified nation, it is not Christianity: Christianity will produce a healthy community; but if it is accepted in order to produce a healthy community, it is not Christianity: Christianity will promote international peace; but if it is accepted in order to promote international peace, it is not Christianity. Our Lord said: "Seek ye first the Kingdom of God and His righteousness, and all these things shall be added unto you." But if you seek first the Kingdom of God and His righteousness *in order that* all those other things may be added unto you, you will miss both those other things and the Kingdom of God as well.

But if Christianity be directed toward another world, if it be a way by which individuals can escape from the present evil age to some better country, what becomes of "the social gospel"? At this point is detected one of the most obvious lines of cleavage between Christianity and the liberal Church. The older evangelism, says the modern liberal preacher, sought to rescue individuals, while the newer evangelism seeks to transform the whole organism of society: the older evangelism was individual; the newer evangelism is social.

This formulation of the issue is not entirely correct, but it contains an element of truth. It is true that historic Christianity is in conflict at many points with the collectivism of the present day; it does emphasize, against the claims of society, the worth of the individual soul. It provides for the individual a refuge from all the fluctuating currents of human opinion, a secret place of meditation where a man can come alone into the presence of God. It does give a man courage to stand, if need be, against the world; it resolutely refuses to make of the individual a mere means to an end, a mere element in the composition of society. It rejects altogether any means of salvation which deals with men in a mass; it brings the individual face to face with his God. In that sense, it is true that Christianity is individualistic and not social.

But though Christianity is individualistic, it is not only individualistic. It provides fully for the social needs of man.

In the first place, even the communion of the individual man with God is not really individualistic, but social. A man is not isolated when he is in communion with God; he can be regarded as isolated only by one who has forgotten the real existence of the supreme Person. Here again, as at many other places, the line of cleavage between liberalism and Christianity really reduces to a profound difference in the conception of God. Christianity is earnestly theistic; liberalism is at best but half-heartedly so. If a man once comes to believe in a personal God, then the worship of Him will not be regarded as selfish isolation, but as the chief end of man. That does not mean that on the Christian view the worship of God is ever to be carried on to the neglect of service rendered to one's fellow-men—"he that loveth not his brother whom he hath seen, is not able to love God whom he hath not seen"—but it does mean that the worship of God has a value of its own. Very different is the prevailing doctrine of modern liberalism. According to Christian belief, man exists for the sake of God; according to the liberal Church, in practice if not in theory, God exists for the sake of man.

But the social element in Christianity is found not only in communion between man and God, but also in communion between man and man. Such communion appears even in institutions which are not specifically Christian.

The most important of such institutions, according to Christian teaching, is the family. And that institution is being pushed more and more into the background. It is being pushed into the background by undue encroachments of the community and of the state. Modern life is tending more and more toward the contraction of the sphere of parental control and parental influence. The choice of schools is being placed under the power of the state; the "community" is seizing hold of recreation and of social activities. It may be a question how far these community activities are responsible for the modern breakdown of the home; very possibly they are only trying to fill a void which even apart from them had already appeared. But the result at any rate is plain—the lives of children are no longer surrounded by the loving atmosphere of the Christian home, but by the utilitarianism of the state. A revival of the Christian religion would unquestionably bring a reversal of the process; the family, as over against all other social institutions, would come to its rights again.

But the state, even when reduced to its proper limits, has a large place in human life, and in the possession of that place it is supported by Christianity. The support, moreover, is independent of the Christian or non-Christian character of the state; it was in the Roman Empire under

Nero that Paul said, "The powers that be are ordained
of God." Christianity assumes no negative attitude,
therefore, toward the state, but recognizes, under existing
conditions, the necessity of government.

The case is similar with respect to those broad aspects
of human life which are associated with industrialism.
The "otherworldliness" of Christianity involves no withdrawal from the battle of this world; our Lord Himself,
with His stupendous mission, lived in the midst of life's
throng and press. Plainly, then, the Christian man may
not simplify his problem by withdrawing from the business
of the world, but must learn to apply the principles of
Jesus even to the complex problems of modern industrial
life. At this point Christian teaching is in full accord
with the modern liberal Church; the evangelical Christian
is not true to his profession if he leaves his Christianity
behind him on Monday morning. On the contrary, the
whole of life, including business and all of social relations,
must be made obedient to the law of love. The Christian
man certainly should display no lack of interest in
"applied Christianity."

Only—and here emerges the enormous difference of
opinion—the Christian man believes that there can be no
applied Christianity unless there be "a Christianity to
apply." [1] That is where the Christian man differs from
the modern liberal. The liberal believes that applied
Christianity is all there is of Christianity, Christianity
being merely a way of life; the Christian man believes
that applied Christianity is the result of an initial act of
God. Thus there is an enormous difference between the
modern liberal and the Christian man with reference to

[1] Francis Shunk Downs, "Christianity and Today," in *Princeton
Theological Review*, xx, 1922, p. 287. See also the whole article, *ibid.*,
pp. 287-304.

human institutions like the community and the state, and with reference to human efforts at applying the Golden Rule in industrial relationships. The modern liberal is optimistic with reference to these institutions; the Christian man is pessimistic unless the institutions be manned by Christian men. The modern liberal believes that human nature as at present constituted can be molded by the principles of Jesus; the Christian man believes that evil can only be held in check and not destroyed by human institutions, and that there must be a transformation of the human materials before any new building can be produced. This difference is not a mere difference in theory, but makes itself felt everywhere in the practical realm. It is particularly evident on the mission field. The missionary of liberalism seeks to spread the blessings of Christian civilization (whatever that may be), and is not particularly interested in leading individuals to relinquish their pagan beliefs. The Christian missionary, on the other hand, regards satisfaction with a mere influence of Christian civilization as a hindrance rather than a help; his chief business, he believes, is the saving of souls, and souls are saved not by the mere ethical principles of Jesus but by His redemptive work. The Christian missionary, in other words, and the Christian worker at home as well as abroad, unlike the apostle of liberalism, says to all men everywhere: "Human goodness will avail nothing for lost souls; ye must be born again."

CHAPTER VII

It has just been observed that Christianity, as well as liberalism, is interested in social institutions. But the most important institution has not yet been mentioned—it is the institution of the Church. When, according to Christian belief, lost souls are saved, the saved ones become united in the Christian Church. It is only by a baseless caricature that Christian missionaries are represented as though they had no interest in education or in the maintenance of a social life in this world; it is not true that they are interested only in saving individual souls and when the souls are saved leave them to their own devices. On the contrary true Christians must everywhere be united in the brotherhood of the Christian Church.

Very different is this Christian conception of brotherhood from the liberal doctrine of the "brotherhood of man." The modern liberal doctrine is that all men everywhere, no matter what their race or creed, are brothers. There is a sense in which this doctrine can be accepted by the Christian. The relation in which all men stand to one another is analogous in some important respects to the relation of brotherhood. All men have the same Creator and the same nature. The Christian man can accept all that the modern liberal means by the brotherhood of man. But the Christian knows also of a relationship far more intimate than that general relationship of man to man.

157

and it is for this more intimate relationship that he reserves the term "brother." The true brotherhood, according to Christian teaching, is the brotherhood of the redeemed.

There is nothing narrow about such teaching; for the Christian brotherhood is open without distinction to all; and the Christian man seeks to bring all men in. Christian service, it is true, is not limited to the household of faith; all men, whether Christians or not, are our neighbors if they be in need. But if we really love our fellowmen we shall never be content with binding up their wounds or pouring on oil and wine or rendering them any such lesser service. We shall indeed do such things for them. But the main business of our lives will be to bring them to the Saviour of their souls.

It is upon this brotherhood of twice-born sinners, this brotherhood of the redeemed, that the Christian founds the hope of society. He finds no solid hope in the improvement of earthly conditions, or the molding of human institutions under the influence of the Golden Rule. These things indeed are to be welcomed. They may so palliate the symptoms of sin that there may be time to apply the true remedy; they may serve to produce conditions upon the earth favorable to the propagation of the gospel message; they are even valuable for their own sake. But in themselves their value, to the Christian, is certainly small. A solid building cannot be constructed when all the materials are faulty; a blessed society cannot be formed out of men who are still under the curse of sin. Human institutions are really to be molded, not by Christian principles accepted by the unsaved, but by Christian men; the true transformation of society will come by the influence of those who have themselves been redeemed.

Thus Christianity differs from liberalism in the way in

which the transformation of society is conceived. But according to Christian belief, as well as according to liberalism, there is really to be a transformation of society; it is not true that the Christian evangelist is interested in the salvation of individuals without being interested in the salvation of the race. And even before the salvation of all society has been achieved, there is already a society of those who have been saved. That society is the Church. The Church is the highest Christian answer to the social needs of man.

And the Church invisible, the true company of the redeemed, finds expression in the companies of Christians who constitute the visible Church to-day. But what is the trouble with the visible Church? What is the reason for its obvious weakness? There are perhaps many causes of weakness. But one cause is perfectly plain—the Church of to-day has been unfaithful to her Lord by admitting great companies of non-Christian persons, not only into her membership, but into her teaching agencies. It is indeed inevitable that some persons who are not truly Christian shall find their way into the visible Church; fallible men cannot discern the heart, and many a profession of faith which seems to be genuine may really be false. But it is not this kind of error to which we now refer. What is now meant is not the admission of individuals whose confessions of faith may not be sincere, but the admission of great companies of persons who have never made any really adequate confession of faith at all and whose entire attitude toward the gospel is the very reverse of the Christian attitude. Such persons, moreover, have been admitted not merely to the membership, but to the ministry of the Church, and to an increasing extent have been allowed to dominate its councils and determine its teaching. The greatest menace to the Christian Church to-day comes not from the enemies outside, but from the enemies within; it comes from the presence within the Church of a type of faith and practice that is anti-Christian to the core.

We are not dealing here with delicate personal questions; we are not presuming to say whether such and such an individual man is a Christian or not. God only can decide such questions; no man can say with assurance whether the attitude of certain individual "liberals" toward Christ is saving faith or not. But one thing is perfectly plain—whether or no liberals are Christians, it is at any rate perfectly clear that liberalism is not Christianity. And that being the case, it is highly undesirable that liberalism and Christianity should continue to be propagated within the bounds of the same organization. A separation between the two parties in the Church is the crying need of the hour.

Many indeed are seeking to avoid the separation. Why, they say, may not brethren dwell together in unity? The Church, we are told, has room both for liberals and for conservatives. The conservatives may be allowed to remain if they will keep trifling matters in the background and attend chiefly to "the weightier matters of the law." And among the things thus designated as "trifling" is found the Cross of Christ, as a really vicarious atonement for sin.

Such obscuration of the issue attests a really astonishing narrowness on the part of the liberal preacher. Narrowness does not consist in definite devotion to certain convictions or in definite rejection of others. But the narrow man is the man who rejects the other man's convictions without first endeavoring to understand them, the man who makes no effort to look at things from the other man's point of view. For example, it is not narrow to

reject the Roman Catholic doctrine that there is no salvation outside the Church. It is not narrow to try to
convince Roman Catholics that that doctrine is wrong.
But it would be very narrow to say to a Roman Catholic:
"You may go on holding your doctrine about the Church
and I shall hold mine, but let us unite in our Christian
work, since despite such trifling differences we are agreed
about the matters that concern the welfare of the soul."
For of course such an utterance would simply beg the
question; the Roman Catholic could not possibly both
hold his doctrine of the Church and at the same time
reject it, as would be required by the program of Church
unity just suggested. A Protestant who would speak in
that way would be narrow, because quite independent of
the question whether he or the Roman Catholic is right
about the Church he would show plainly that he had not
made the slightest effort to understand the Roman
Catholic point of view.

The case is similar with the liberal program for unity
in the Church. It could never be advocated by anyone
who had made the slightest effort to understand the point
of view of his opponent in the controversy. The liberal
preacher says to the conservative party in the Church:
"Let us unite in the same congregation, since of course
doctrinal differences are trifles." But it is the very
essence of "conservatism" in the Church to regard doctrinal differences as no trifles but as the matters of
supreme moment. A man cannot possibly be an "evangelical" or a "conservative" (or, as he himself would say,
simply a Christian) and regard the Cross of Christ as a
trifle. To suppose that he can is the extreme of narrowness. It is not necessarily "narrow" to reject the vicarious sacrifice of our Lord as the sole means of salvation.
It may be very wrong (and we believe that it is), but it is

not necessarily narrow. But to suppose that a man can hold to the vicarious sacrifice of Christ and at the same time belittle that doctrine, to suppose that a man can believe that the eternal Son of God really bore the guilt of men's sins on the Cross and at the same time regard that belief as a "trifle" without bearing upon the welfare of men's souls—that is very narrow and very absurd. We shall really get nowhere in this controversy unless we make a sincere effort to understand the other man's point of view.

But for another reason also the effort to sink doctrinal differences and unite the Church on a program of Christian service is unsatisfactory. It is unsatisfactory because, in its usual contemporary form, it is dishonest. Whatever may be thought of Christian doctrine, it can hardly be denied that honesty is one of the "weightier matters of the law." Yet honesty is being relinquished in wholesale fashion by the liberal party in many ecclesiastical bodies to-day.

To recognize that fact one does not need to take sides at all with regard to the doctrinal or historical questions. Suppose it be true that devotion to a creed is a sign of narrowness or intolerance, suppose the Church ought to be founded upon devotion to the ideal of Jesus or upon the desire to put His spirit into operation in the world, and not at all upon a confession of faith with regard to His redeeming work. Even if all this were true, even if a creedal Church were an undesirable thing, it would still remain true that as a matter of fact many (indeed in spirit really all) evangelical churches are creedal churches, and that if a man does not accept their creed he has no right to a place in their teaching ministry. The creedal character of the churches is differently expressed in the different evangelical bodies, but the example of the Presbyterian Church in the United States of America may perhaps serve to illustrate what is meant. It is required of all officers in the Presbyterian Church, including the ministers, that at their ordination they make answer "plainly" to a series of questions which begins with the two following:

"Do you believe the Scriptures of the Old and New Testaments to be the Word of God, the only infallible rule of faith and practice?"

"Do you sincerely receive and adopt the Confession of Faith of this Church, as containing the system of doctrine taught in the Holy Scriptures?"

If these "constitutional questions" do not fix clearly the creedal basis of the Presbyterian Church, it is difficult to see how any human language could possibly do so. Yet immediately after making such a solemn declaration, immediately after declaring that the Westminster Confession contains the system of doctrine taught in infallible Scriptures, many ministers of the Presbyterian Church will proceed to decry that same Confession and that doctrine of the infallibility of Scripture to which they have just solemnly subscribed!

We are not now speaking of the membership of the Church, but of the ministry, and we are not speaking of the man who is troubled by grave doubts and wonders whether with his doubts he can honestly continue his membership in the Church. For great hosts of such troubled souls the Church offers bountifully its fellowship and its aid; it would be a crime to cast them out. There are many men of little faith in our troublous times. It is not of them that we speak. God grant that they may obtain comfort and help through the ministrations of the Church!

But we are speaking of men very different from these

men of little faith—from these men who are troubled by
doubts and are seeking earnestly for the truth. The men
whom we mean are seeking not membership in the Church,
but a place in the ministry, and they desire not to learn
but to teach. They are not men who say, "I believe, help
mine unbelief," but men who are proud in the possession
of the knowledge of this world, and seek a place in the
ministry that they may teach what is directly contrary to
the Confession of Faith to which they subscribe. For that
course of action various excuses are made—the growth of
custom by which the constitutional questions are supposed
to have become a dead letter, various mental reservations,
various "interpretations" of the declaration (which of
course mean a complete reversal of the meaning). But no
such excuses can change the essential fact. Whether it
be desirable or not, the ordination declaration is part of
the constitution of the Church. If a man can stand on
that platform he may be an officer in the Presbyterian
Church; if he cannot stand on it he has no right to be an
officer in the Presbyterian Church. And the case is no
doubt essentially similar in other evangelical Churches.
Whether we like it or not, these Churches are founded
upon a creed; they are organized for the propagation of
a message. If a man desires to combat that message
instead of propagating it, he has no right, no matter how
false the message may be, to gain a vantage ground for
combating it by making a declaration of his faith which
—be it plainly spoken—is not true.

But if such a course of action is wrong, another course
of action is perfectly open to the man who desires to
propagate "liberal Christianity." Finding the existing
"evangelical" churches to be bound up to a creed which
he does not accept, he may either unite himself with some
other existing body or else found a new body to suit him-

self. There are of course certain obvious disadvantages in such a course—the abandonment of church buildings to which one is attached, the break in family traditions, the injury to sentiment of various kinds. But there is one supreme advantage which far overbalances all such disadvantages. It is the advantage of honesty. The path of honesty in such matters may be rough and thorny, but it can be trod. And it has already been trod—for example, by the Unitarian Church. The Unitarian Church is frankly and honestly just the kind of church that the liberal preacher desires—namely, a church without an authoritative Bible, without doctrinal requirements, and without a creed.

Honesty, despite all that can be said and done, is not a trifle, but one of the weightier matters of the law. Certainly it has a value of its own, a value quite independent of consequences. But the consequences of honesty would in the case now under discussion not be unsatisfactory; here as elsewhere honesty would probably prove to be the best policy. By withdrawing from the confessional churches—those churches that are founded upon a creed derived from Scripture—the liberal preacher would indeed sacrifice the opportunity, almost within his grasp, of so obtaining control of those confessional churches as to change their fundamental character. The sacrifice of that opportunity would mean that the hope of turning the resources of the evangelical churches into the propagation of liberalism would be gone. But liberalism would certainly not suffer in the end. There would at least be no more need of using equivocal language, no more need of avoiding offence. The liberal preacher would obtain the full personal respect even of his opponents, and the whole discussion would be placed on higher ground. All would be perfectly straightforward and above-board. And if liberalism is true, the mere loss of physical resources would not prevent it from making its way.

At this point a question may arise. If there ought to be a separation between the liberals and the conservatives in the Church, why should not the conservatives be the ones to withdraw? Certainly it may come to that. If the liberal party really obtains full control of the councils of the Church, then no evangelical Christian can continue to support the Church's work. If a man believes that salvation from sin comes only through the atoning death of Jesus, then he cannot honestly support by his gifts and by his presence a propaganda which is intended to produce an exactly opposite impression. To do so would mean the most terrible bloodguiltiness which it is possible to conceive. If the liberal party, therefore, really obtains control of the Church, evangelical Christians must be prepared to withdraw no matter what it costs. Our Lord has died for us, and surely we must not deny Him for favor of men. But up to the present time such a situation has not yet appeared; the creedal basis still stands firm in the constitutions of evangelical churches. And there is a very real reason why it is not the "conservatives" who ought to withdraw. The reason is found in the trust which the churches hold. That trust includes trust funds of the most definite kind. And contrary to what seems to be the prevailing opinion, we venture to regard a trust as a sacred thing. The funds of the evangelical churches are held under a very definite trust; they are committed to the various bodies for the propagation of the gospel as set forth in the Bible and in the confessions of faith. To devote them to any other purpose, even though that other purpose should be in itself far more desirable, would be a violation of trust.

It must be admitted that the present situation is anomalous. Funds dedicated to the propagation of the gospel by godly men and women of previous generations or given by thoroughly evangelical congregations to-day are in nearly all the churches being used *partly* in the propagation of what is diametrically opposed to the evangelical faith. Certainly that situation ought not to continue; it is an offence to every thoughtfully honest man whether he be Christian or not. But in remaining in the existing churches the conservatives are in a fundamentally different position from the liberals; for the conservatives are in agreement with the plain constitutions of the churches, while the liberal party can maintain itself only by an equivocal subscription to declarations which it does not really believe.

But how shall so anomalous a situation be brought to an end? The best way would undoubtedly be the voluntary withdrawal of the liberal ministers from those confessional churches whose confessions they do not, in the plain historical sense, accept. And we have not altogether abandoned hope of such a solution. Our differences with the liberal party in the Church are indeed profound, but with regard to the obligation of simple honesty of speech, some agreement might surely be attained. Certainly the withdrawal of liberal ministers from the creedal churches would be enormously in the interests of harmony and co-operation. Nothing engenders strife so much as a forced unity, within the same organization, of those who disagree fundamentally in aim.

But is not advocacy of such separation a flagrant instance of intolerance? The objection is often raised. But it ignores altogether the difference between involuntary and voluntary organizations. Involuntary organizations ought to be tolerant, but voluntary organizations, so far as the fundamental purpose of their existence is concerned, must be intolerant or else cease to exist. The state is an involuntary organization; a man is forced to be a member of it whether he will or no. It is therefore an interference with liberty for the state to prescribe any one type of opinion or any one type of education for its citizens. But within the state, individual citizens who desire to unite for some special purpose should be permitted to do so. Especially in the sphere of religion, such permission of individuals to unite is one of the rights which lie at the very foundation of our civil and religious liberty. The state does not scrutinize the rightness or wrongness of the religious purpose for which such voluntary religious associations are formed—if it did undertake such scrutiny all religious liberty would be gone—but it merely protects the right of individuals to unite for any religious purpose which they may choose.

Among such voluntary associations are to be found the evangelical churches. An evangelical church is composed of a number of persons who have come to agreement in a certain message about Christ and who desire to unite in the propagation of that message, as it is set forth in their creed on the basis of the Bible. No one is forced to unite himself with the body thus formed; and because of this total absence of compulsion there can be no interference with liberty in the maintenance of any specific purpose— for example, the propagation of a message—as a fundamental purpose of the association. If other persons desire to form a religious association with some purpose other than the propagation of a message—for example, the purpose of promoting in the world, simply by exhortation and by the inspiration of the example of Jesus, a certain type of life—they are at perfect liberty to do so. But for an organization which is founded with the fundamental purpose of propagating a message to commit its resources and its name to those who are engaged in combating the message is not tolerance but simple dishonesty. Yet it is exactly this course of action that is advocated by those who would allow non-doctrinal religion to be taught in the name of doctrinal churches—churches that are plainly doctrinal both in their constitutions and in the declarations which they require of every candidate for ordination.

The matter may be made plain by an illustration from secular life. Suppose in a political campaign in America there be formed a Democratic club for the purpose of furthering the cause of the Democratic party. Suppose there are certain other citizens who are opposed to the tenets of the Democratic club and in opposition desire to support the Republican party. What is the honest way for them to accomplish their purpose? Plainly it is simply the formation of a Republican club which shall carry on a propaganda in favor of Republican principles. But suppose, instead of pursuing this simple course of action, the advocates of Republican principles should conceive the notion of making a declaration of conformity to Democratic principles, thus gaining an entrance into the Democratic club and finally turning its resources into an anti-Democratic propaganda. That plan might be ingenious. But would it be honest? Yet it is just exactly such a plan which is adopted by advocates of a non-doctrinal religion who by subscription to a creed gain an entrance into the teaching ministry of doctrinal or evangelical churches. Let no one be offended by the illustration taken from ordinary life. We are not for a moment suggesting that the Church is no more than a political club. But the fact that the Church is more than a political club does not mean that in ecclesiastical affairs there is any abrogation of the homely principles of honesty.

The Church may possibly be more honest, but certainly it ought not to be less honest, than a political club.

Certainly the essentially creedal character of evangelical churches is firmly fixed. A man may disagree with the Westminster Confession, for example, but he can hardly fail to see what it means; at least he can hardly fail to understand the "system of doctrine" which is taught in it. The Confession, whatever its faults may be, is certainly not lacking in definiteness. And certainly a man who solemnly accepts that system of doctrine as his own cannot at the same time be an advocate of a non-doctrinal religion which regards as a trifling thing that which is the very sum and substance of the Confession and the very centre and core of the Bible upon which it is based. Similar is the case in other evangelical churches The Protestant Episcopal Church, some of whose members, it is true, might resent the distinctive title of "evangelical," is clearly founded upon a creed, and that creed, including the exultant supernaturalism of the New Testament and the redemption offered by Christ, is plainly involved in the Book of Common Prayer which every priest in his own name and in the name of the congregation must read.

The separation of naturalistic liberalism from the evangelical churches would no doubt greatly diminish the size of the churches. But Gideon's three hundred were more powerful than the thirty-two thousand with which the march against the Midianites began.

Certainly the present situation is fraught with deadly weakness. Christian men have been redeemed from sin, without merit of their own, by the sacrifice of Christ. But every man who has been truly redeemed from sin longs to carry to others the same blessed gospel through which he himself has been saved. The propagation of the gospe, is clearly the joy as well as the duty of every Christian man. But how shall the gospel be propagated? The natural answer is that it shall be propagated through the agencies of the Church—boards of missions and the like. An obvious duty, therefore, rests upon the Christian man of contributing to the agencies of the Church. But at this point the perplexity arises. The Christian man discovers to his consternation that the agencies of the Church are propagating not only the gospel as found in the Bible and in the historic creeds, but also a type of religious teaching which is at every conceivable point the diametrical opposite of the gospel. The question naturally arises whether there is any reason for contributing to such agencies at all. Of every dollar contributed to them, perhaps half goes to the support of true missionaries of the Cross, while the other half goes to the support of those who are persuading men that the message of the Cross is unnecessary or wrong. If part of our gifts is to be used to neutralize the other part, is not contribution to mission boards altogether absurd? The question may at least very naturally be raised. It should not indeed be answered hastily in a way hostile to contribution to mission boards. Perhaps it is better that the gospel should be both preached and combated by the same agencies than that it should not be preached at all. At any rate, the true missionaries of the Cross, even though the mission boards which support them should turn out to be very bad, must not be allowed to be in want. But the situation, from the point of view of the evangelical Christian, is unsatisfactory in the extreme. Many Christians seek to relieve the situation by "designating" their gifts, instead of allowing them to be distributed by the mission agencies. But at this point one encounters the centralization of power which is going on in the modern Church. On account of that centralization the designation of gifts is often found to be illusory. If gifts are devoted by the donors to one mission known to be evangelical, that does not always really increase the resources of that mission; for the mission boards can simply cut down the proportion assigned to that mission from the undesignated funds, and the final result is exactly the same as if there had been no designation of the gift at all.

The existence and the necessity of mission boards and the like prevents, in general, one obvious solution of the present difficulty in the Church—the solution offered by local autonomy of the congregation. It might be suggested that each congregation should determine its own confession of faith or its own program of work. Then each congregation might seem to be responsible only for itself, and might seem to be relieved from the odious task of judging others. But the suggestion is impracticable. Aside from the question whether a purely congregational system of church government is desirable in itself, it is impossible where mission agencies are concerned. In the support of such agencies, many congregations obviously must unite; and the question arises whether evangelical congregations can honestly support agencies which are opposed to the evangelical faith.

At any rate, the situation cannot be helped by ignoring facts. The plain fact is that liberalism, whether it be true or false, is no mere "heresy"—no mere divergence at isolated points from Christian teaching. On the contrary it proceeds from a totally different root, and it constitutes, in essentials, a unitary system of its own. That does not mean that all liberals hold all parts of the system, or that Christians who have been affected by liberal teaching at one point have been affected at all points. There is sometimes a salutary lack of logic which prevents the whole of a man's faith being destroyed when he has given up a part. But the true way in which to examine a spiritual movement is in its logical relations; logic is the great dynamic, and the logical implications of any way of thinking are sooner or later certain to be worked out. And taken as a whole, even as it actually exists to-day, naturalistic liberalism is a fairly unitary phenomenon; it is tending more and more to eliminate from itself illogical remnants of Christian belief. It differs from Christianity in its view of God, of man, of the seat of authority and of the way of salvation. And it differs from Christianity not only in theology but in the whole of life. It is indeed sometimes said that there can be communion in feeling where communion in thinking is gone, a communion of the heart as distinguished from a communion of the head. But with respect to the present controversy, such a distinction certainly does not apply. On the contrary, in reading the books and listening to the sermons of recent liberal teachers—so untroubled by the problem of sin, so devoid of all sympathy for guilty humanity, so prone to abuse and ridicule the things dearest to the heart of every Christian man—one can only confess that if liberalism is to return into the Christian communion there must be a change of heart fully as much as a change of mind. God grant that such a change of heart may come! But meanwhile the present situation must not be ignored but faced. Christianity is being attacked from within by a movement which is anti-Christian to the core.

What is the duty of Christian men at such at time? What is the duty, in particular, of Christian officers in the Church?

In the first place, they should encourage those who are engaging in the intellectual and spiritual struggle. They should not say, in the sense in which some laymen say it, that more time should be devoted to the propagation of Christianity, and less to the defence of Christianity. Certainly there should be propagation of Christianity. Believers should certainly not content themselves with warding off attacks, but should also unfold in an orderly and positive way the full riches of the gospel. But far more is usually meant by those who call for less defence and more propagation. What they really intend is the discouragement of the whole intellectual defence of the faith. And their words come as a blow in the face of those who are fighting the great battle. As a matter of fact, not less time, but more time, should be devoted to the defence of the gospel. Indeed, truth cannot be stated clearly at all without being set over against error. Thus a large part of the New Testament is polemic; the enunciation of evangelical truth was occasioned by the errors which had arisen in the churches. So it will always be, on account of the fundamental laws of the human mind. Moreover, the present crisis must be taken into account. There may have been a day when there could be propagation of Christianity without defence. But such a day at any rate is past. At the present time, when the opponents of the gospel are almost in control of our churches, the slightest avoidance of the defence of the gospel is just sheer unfaithfulness to the Lord. There have been previous great crises in the history of the Church, crises almost comparable to this. One appeared in the second century, when the very life of Christendom was threatened by the Gnostics. Another came in the Middle Ages when the gospel of God's grace seemed forgotten. In such times of crisis, God has always saved the Church. But He has always saved it not by theological pacifists, but by sturdy contenders for the truth.

In the second place, Christian officers in the Church

should perform their duty in deciding upon the qualifications of candidates for the ministry. The question "For Christ or against him?" constantly arises in the examination of candidates for ordination. Attempts are often made to obscure the issue. It is often said: "The candidate will no doubt move in the direction of the truth; let him now be sent out to learn as well as to preach." And so another opponent of the gospel enters the councils of the Church, and another false prophet goes forth to encourage sinners to come before the judgment seat of God clad in the miserable rags of their own righteousness. Such action is not really "kind" to the candidate himself. It is never kind to encourage a man to enter into a life of dishonesty. The fact often seems to be forgotten that the evangelical Churches are purely voluntary organizations; no one is required to enter into their service. If a man cannot accept the belief of such churches, there are other ecclesiastical bodies in which he can find a place. The belief of the Presbyterian Church, for example, is plainly set forth in the Confession of Faith, and the Church will never afford any warmth of communion or engage with any real vigor in her work until her ministers are in whole-hearted agreement with that belief. It is strange how in the interests of an utterly false kindness to men, Christians are sometimes willing to relinquish their loyalty to the crucified Lord.

In the third place, Christian officers in the Church should show their loyalty to Christ in their capacity as members of the individual congregations. The issue often arises in connection with the choice of a pastor. Such and such a man, it is said, is a brilliant preacher. But what is the content of his preaching? Is his preaching full of the gospel of Christ? The answer is often evasive. The preacher in question, it is said, is of good standing in the

Church, and he has never denied the doctrines or grace. Therefore, it is urged, he should be called to the pastorate. But shall we be satisfied with such negative assurances? Shall we be satisfied with preachers who merely "do not deny" the Cross of Christ? God grant that such satisfaction may be broken down! The people are perishing under the ministrations of those who "do not deny" the Cross of Christ. Surely something more than that is needed. God send us ministers who, instead of merely avoiding denial of the Cross shall be on fire with the Cross, whose whole life shall be one burning sacrifice of gratitude to the blessed Saviour who loved them and gave Himself for them!

In the fourth place—the most important thing of all— there must be a renewal of Christian education. The rejection of Christianity is due to various causes. But a very potent cause is simple ignorance. In countless cases, Christianity is rejected simply because men have not the slightest notion of what Christianity is. An outstanding fact of recent Church history is the appalling growth of ignorance in the Church. Various causes, no doubt, can be assigned for this lamentable development. The development is due partly to the general decline of education— at least so far as literature and history are concerned. The schools of the present day are being ruined by the absurd notion that education should follow the line of least resistance, and that something can be "drawn out" of the mind before anything is put in. They are also being ruined by an exaggerated emphasis on methodology at the expense of content and on what is materially useful at the expense of the high spiritual heritage of mankind. These lamentable tendencies, moreover, are in danger of being made permanent through the sinister extension of state control. But something more than the general decline in education is needed to account for the special growth of ignorance in the Church. The growth of ignorance in the Church is the logical and inevitable result of the false notion that Christianity is a life and not also a doctrine; if Christianity is not a doctrine then of course teaching is not necessary to Christianity. But whatever be the causes for the growth of ignorance in the Church, the evil must be remedied. It must be remedied primarily by the renewal of Christian education in the family, but also by the use of whatever other educational agencies the Church can find. Christian education is the chief business of the hour for every earnest Christian man. Christianity cannot subsist unless men know what Christianity is; and the fair and logical thing is to learn what Christianity is, not from its opponents, but from those who themselves are Christians. That method of procedure would be the only fair method in the case of any movement. But it is still more in place in the case of a movement such as Christianity which has laid the foundation of all that we hold most dear. Men have abundant opportunity to-day to learn what can be said against Christianity, and it is only fair that they should also learn something about the thing that is being attacked.

Such measures are needed to-day. The present is a time not for ease or pleasure, but for earnest and prayerful work. A terrible crisis unquestionably has arisen in the Church. In the ministry of evangelical churches are to be found hosts of those who reject the gospel of Christ. By the equivocal use of traditional phrases, by the representation of differences of opinion as though they were only differences about the interpretation of the Bible, entrance into the Church was secured for those who are hostile to the very foundations of the faith.

And now there are some indications that the fiction of conformity to the past is to be thrown off, and the real meaning of what has been taking place is to be allowed to appear. The Church, it is now apparently supposed, has almost been educated up to the point where the shackles of the Bible can openly be cast away and the doctrine of the Cross of Christ can be relegated to the limbo of discarded subtleties.

Yet there is in the Christian life no room for despair. Only, our hopefulness should not be founded on the sand. It should be founded, not upon a blind ignorance of the danger, but solely upon the precious promises of God. Laymen, as well as ministers, should return, in these trying days, with new earnestness, to the study of the Word of God.

If the Word of God be heeded, the Christian battle will be fought both with love and with faithfulness. Party passions and personal animosities will be put away, but on the other hand, even angels from heaven will be rejected if they preach a gospel different from the blessed gospel of the Cross. Every man must decide upon which side he will stand. God grant that we may decide aright!

What the immediate future may bring we cannot presume to say. The final result indeed is clear. God has not deserted His Church; He has brought her through even darker hours than those which try our courage now, yet the darkest hour has always come before the dawn. We have to-day the entrance of paganism into the Church in the name of Christianity. But in the second century a similar battle was fought and won. From another point of view, modern liberalism is like the legalism of the middle ages, with its dependence upon the merit of man. And another Reformation in God's good time will come.

But meanwhile our souls are tried. We can only try to

do our duty in humility and in sole reliance upon the Saviour who bought us with His blood. The future is in God's hand, and we do not know the means that He will use in the accomplishment of His will. It may be that the present evangelical churches will face the facts, and regain their integrity while yet there is time. If that solution is to be adopted there is no time to lose, since the forces opposed to the gospel are now almost in control. It is possible that the existing churches may be given over altogether to naturalism, that men may then see that the fundamental needs of the soul are to be satisfied not inside but outside of the existing churches, and that thus new Christian groups may be formed.

But whatever solution there may be, one thing is clear. There must be somewhere groups of redeemed men and women who can gather together humbly in the name of Christ, to give thanks to Him for His unspeakable gift and to worship the Father through Him. Such groups alone can satisfy the needs of the soul. At the present time, there is one longing of the human heart which is often forgotten—it is the deep, pathetic longing of the Christian for fellowship with his brethren. One hears much, it is true, about Christian union and harmony and co-operation. But the union that is meant is often a union with the world against the Lord, or at best a forced union of machinery and tyrannical committees. How different is the true unity of the Spirit in the bond of peace! Sometimes, it is true, the longing for Christian fellowship is satisfied. There are congregations, even in the present age of conflict, that are really gathered around the table of the crucified Lord; there are pastors that are pastors indeed. But such congregations, in many cities, are difficult to find. Weary with the conflicts of the world, one goes into the Church to seek refreshment for the soul.

And what does one find? Alas, too often, one finds only
the turmoil of the world. The preacher comes forward,
not out of a secret place of meditation and power, not
with the authority of God's Word permeating his message,
not with human wisdom pushed far into the background
by the glory of the Cross, but with human opinions about
the social problems of the hour or easy solutions of the
vast problem of sin. Such is the sermon. And then perhaps the service is closed by one of those hymns breathing
out the angry passions of 1861, which are to be found
in the back part of the hymnals. Thus the warfare of
the world has entered even into the house of God, And
sad indeed is the heart of the man who has come seeking
peace.

Is there no refuge from strife? Is there no place of
refreshing where a man can prepare for the battle of life?
Is there no place where two or three can gather in Jesus'
name, to forget for the moment all those things that divide
nation from nation and race from race, to forget human
pride, to forget the passions of war, to forget the puzzling
problems of industrial strife, and to unite in overflowing
gratitude at the foot of the Cross? If there be such a
place, then that is the house of God and that the gate of
heaven. And from under the threshold of that house will
go forth a river that will revive the weary world.

INDEX

INDEX

I NAMES AND SUBJECTS

Abbott, Lyman, 23.
America: political changes in, 10-15; schools in, 11-14.
Americanization, 149, 152.
Anglican Church, 51.
Apostles, given authority by Jesus, 76f.
Apostolic succession, doctrine of, 51.
Applied Christianity, 155f.
Arianism, 113.
Arminianism, 51f.
Art, decline in, 10.
Atonement, 117-136: liberal theories of, based upon a lignt view of sin, 119; Christian view of, scorned by liberalism, 119f., 160; Christian view of, criticized on the ground that it makes salvation depend on history, 120-122, that it limits salvation, 122-125, that it involves transference of guilt from one person to another, 125-129, that it involves a low view of the love of God, 129-135; Christian doctrine of, necessity of earnest devotion to, 175f.; atonement was made by God Himself, 132.
Authority: the seat of, 75-79; of Jesus, not really accepted by liberalism, 76-78.

Bengel, 139.
Bible, the: Christian and liberal views of, contrasted, 69-79; reiterates the presuppositions of

the gospel, 69; contains an account of a redeeming event, 69-72; forms the basis for the creeds, 163, 165.
Bolshevism, 150f.
Bousset, 82.
Brotherhood, 18f.; Christian and liberal views of, contrasted, 157f.
Bunyan, John, 46.
Burton, E. D., 144.

Calvin, 45.
Calvinism, 51.
Cause, idea of, 101.
Chamberlain, Houston Stewart, 33.
Chester Presbytery, address delivered before Ruling Elders' Association of, vii.
Chiliasm, 49.
Christianity: modern presumption against, 4; relation of, to science, 4-7; is it a life as distinguished from a doctrine, 19-53; fundamental nature of, determined by its beginnings, 20-45; was at its inception a life founded upon a message, 21; cannot be treated as a mere means to an end, 151f.; social aspects of, 152-156.
Church, the: responsibility of, 124f.; Christian and liberal views of, contrasted, 157-180; has admitted non-Christian men into teaching agencies, 159f.; need for division in, 160-

183

II BIBLICAL PASSAGES